What others are saying about Reinhard Bonnke and *Raised from the Dead*...

Perhaps no other evangelist has advanced the cause of the gospel as effectively as Reinhard Bonnke has. His crusades throughout Africa have had a legendary impact on the kingdom. In *Raised from the Dead*, Pastor Bonnke shares how one incredible miracle served as a sign from God that he should bring his extraordinary message of salvation to America. Read it, and prepare to be amazed at what God can do!

—*Pat Robertson*
Chairman of CBN; host, *The 700 Club*

Raised from the Dead reads like a summer blockbuster movie, but it's all true. You'll be amazed at what God can do through an obedient man under the anointing of the Holy Spirit. I heartily endorse both the man and his message.

—*Bill Johnson*
Senior Pastor, Bethel Church, Redding, California
Author, *Hosting the Presence* and *The Supernatural Ways of Royalty*

RAISED
FROM THE
DEAD

REINHARD
BONNKE

WHITAKER
HOUSE

Unless otherwise indicated, all Scripture quotations are taken from the King James Version of the Holy Bible. Scripture reference marked (RSV) is taken from the *Revised Standard Version* of the Bible, © 1946, 1952, and 1971 by the Division of Christian Education of the National Council of the Churches of Christ in the United States of America. Used by permission. All rights reserved.

Boldface type in the Scripture quotations indicates the author's emphasis.

RAISED FROM THE DEAD:
The Miracle That Brings Promise to America

Harvester Services, Inc.
740 Florida Central Pkwy
Suite 2028
Longwood, Florida 32750
www.ReinhardBonnke.com

ISBN: 978-1-60374-952-7
eBook ISBN: 978-1-60374-977-0
Printed in the United States of America
© 2014 by Reinhard Bonnke

Whitaker House
1030 Hunt Valley Circle
New Kensington, PA 15068
www.whitakerhouse.com

Library of Congress Cataloging-in-Publication Data (Pending)

1 2 3 4 5 6 7 8 9 10 11   ᙃ   21 20 19 18 17 16 15 14

CONTENTS

PREFACE

PREFACE

This book begins with a resurrection in Africa, followed by a miracle of deliverance, and concludes with revival in America. When I speak of revival, I am speaking of a mighty awakening, a tidal wave of salvations sweeping across the United States from stadium to stadium, city to city, coast to coast. Perhaps you say in your heart, *Impossible!* I understand. As a struggling young missionary in the small African nation of Lesotho in 1974, I heard the Lord say to me, *Africa shall be saved.* How could I grasp such a word from the Lord? At the time, I was a nameless nobody, seeking to serve the Lord on the "Dark Continent." Such a preposterous word to my ears! Preposterous, *unless God had spoken.* No one could have foreseen it, but since that day, I have registered 74 million decisions for Christ throughout Africa. With that experience behind me, I believe I can say with full assurance that God *did* speak to me in 1974.

Once again, in 2012, I have heard a word from God. He said to me, *America will be saved.* As you will see by the end of this book, the fulfillment of that promise is already in motion. Some will see it and not believe it. These are people of unbelief who will reap what they have sown. Others will believe the words before they see them manifest. The words from God are all that matter to them. They will repeat the phrase "America will be saved" and be willing to make a stand. These are people of faith who will rejoice in the harvest, even before it is fully ripe. I hope that you are among them.

To inspire you, I introduce you in this book to an unlikely hero of faith—an African housewife named Nneka Ekechukwu. The word of God came to her in 2001, and she received in her heart a scriptural promise that she would see her dead husband, Daniel, raised to life again. By faith she reached out and took hold of it. How true was her faith? Before it was over, she stood absolutely alone—assailed, deserted, ridiculed, and clinging to empty air—*unless God had spoken!* I can now say with full assurance that God *did* speak to her in 2001, and His word performed the impossible.

And so, here I tell the story of Nneka's faith in the midst of unbelief. It is part of a larger picture linking the resurrection of her husband in 2001 to God's word to me concerning America in 2012. A decade later, Daniel's resurrection has become a sign to confirm the things I have heard in my spirit.

The trial of Nneka's faith is both a true story and a parable. If you allow it to, it will become a mirror of some hidden places in your soul. You will be like the man with the tormented son to whom Jesus said, *"If thou canst believe, all things are possible"* (Mark 9:23). The word *"If"* was too much for him. Pierced to the core, the man saw his unbelief and burst into tears. *"Lord, I believe; help thou mine unbelief"* (Mark 9:24). Jesus did not rebuke him for this moment of honesty. Quite the opposite. He unleashed His miraculous power to heal the man's son, but only after the man had seen his own heart and had acknowledged that both belief and unbelief struggled within. He chose belief. As you read this story, may God help your unbelief.

As I begin, I would like to explain my use of the term *resurrection* in this book. I am using the term according to its dictionary definition: "the state of one risen from the dead." In theological terms, there has been only one true resurrection, and that is the resurrection of our Lord. In that respect, He is the firstborn from the dead. (See Acts 26:23; Colossians 1:18; Revelation 1:5.)

Jesus' resurrection is unique in that He was raised in His body from the grave, never to die again. He ascended in His physical substance to heaven and returned to earth with a glorified body that was able to appear and disappear. This ability was demonstrated to the disciples on the road to Emmaus (see Luke 24:13–31) and later to the disciples gathered behind closed doors after His death (see John 20:26). His glorified body was capable of many other things that have not been demonstrated, I'm sure. We know, for instance, that John, who laid his head on Jesus' chest at the Last Supper, fell as one dead at the very sight of the glorified Lord in the midst of the seven candlesticks. (See Revelation 1:17–20.) Eye hath not seen a fraction of the wonders of our resurrected Lord.

As you will see in the resurrection of Daniel Ekechukwu, his body never left the earth. Like many others, he tells of an out-of-body trip through heaven and hell. His body was definitely not with him on that journey. Rather, his resurrection was like the raising of Lazarus from the dead. Lazarus eventually had to die again, as it is appointed unto all men to die. (See Hebrews 9:27.) Happily, that is not the end of the resurrection story.

In the full meaning of the word *resurrection*, all of us are scheduled to rise on the last day. Those who have lived and died, from Adam and Eve until the present day, will see their bodies rise from dust and decay to join their souls and spirits in eternity. The body will be changed and glorified. We know only a little of what that might mean. Those who are resurrected to life will join Jesus, the firstborn from the dead, in the realms of heaven, while those who have rejected the sacrifice of God's Son will experience eternal damnation. This is the biblical view, and it is the message I preach.

My reason for using the term *resurrection,* in this case, is to distinguish it from *resuscitation.* There are those who have died briefly and have been medically resuscitated. This is especially true in our era of advanced medical practice. I recently heard of a woman who was resuscitated seven times by an emergency team in Toronto. Their efforts finally resulted in her remaining alive. Some who have been resuscitated have experienced out-of-body journeys similar to Daniel's. But that is not proof that they were truly dead. Some who are in a coma also report out-of-body experiences. In Daniel's case, a great deal of medical evidence suggests that he was far beyond all hope of medical resuscitation. He was totally dead for several days and had been partially embalmed in a mortuary. For that reason, I have chosen to use the word *resurrection* to describe his miracle.

The raising of Daniel from the dead is a story that will offend some people. I can guarantee it. That is one reason I have waited for more than a decade to tell it in my own words. I do not wish to offend anyone. And if offending were the only result of speaking up, I would now remain silent.

I tell of the miracle now because it towers over my life and ministry like the steeple of a great cathedral. It points to the heavens, and to the God I serve. It reminds me in a thousand ways that His mind and His ways are high above my own. (See Isaiah 55:9.) And this is the great offense in the Daniel Ekechukwu story. It may not fit your well-conceived notions of God and how He should act in all circumstances. It may defy some part of your tradition and your understanding. It may push you out of your comfort zone and make the wisdom of the wise seem foolish. (See 1 Corinthians 1:20.) Yes, even the most exalted thoughts of our religious scholars will seem inadequate. There are no human heroes in this story. Every player is flawed and oh so human. It is a story that glorifies God alone, and that is the reason I tell it.

Events like this miracle, though rare, are nothing new. Throughout history God has found the means to humble human intelligence again and again. Man's urge to define God, to contain Him in a theological box, is something that relentlessly exalts itself. I am reminded of that great genius and defender of the Christian faith, Thomas Aquinas, whose writings have inspired the thinking of Christian scholars for centuries. But just before his death in 1274, he received a vision that utterly silenced him. "I can write no more," he said. "I have seen things which make all my writings like straw."[1]

And so, too, my writing about the resurrection of Daniel Ekechukwu is "like straw." It will be nothing next to the full glory we will know when we come face-to-face with our Maker. I am sure that I will not capture the whole of it. Nor will I claim to do so. I will, however, offer my perspective in this book, because God ordained that I play a remarkable role in the miracle. Not the expected role, mind you. And that rings true, does it not? If God met our expectations, He would not exceed our imaginations. As the apostle Paul wrote, *"Eye hath not seen, nor ear heard, neither have entered into the heart of man, the things which God hath prepared for them that love him"* (1 Corinthians 2:9).

Humbly, then, and with that Scripture firmly in mind, I will approach my telling of the event. I believe this miracle has much to teach us about God's love and mercy, and it has become a sign to me of revival coming to America. I am an evangelist. I approach this story as one who leads many to the door of salvation. In my ministry, we have seen many miracles that confirm the preaching of the gospel. This resurrection story, however, seems to stand alone, in a category all by itself.

Finally, I will share a second story about an African man named Richard. I found this man in a primitive prison, living under a death sentence. He was doomed, with no hope of pardon and no means of appeal. When I looked at him, sitting amid a group of condemned men, the word of the Lord came to me, saying, *This man shall be set free!* I declared that very word of the Lord to Richard, even as he was bound in cruel, iron shackles, awaiting the hangman. How could I speak life and release to such a man when I had no power to make it happen? How could I raise his hopes so high when I had not one shred of earthly proof?

As I left that remote African city, Richard remained in his chains, facing what seemed to be certain death. Some feared that I had spoken as

---

1. G. K. Chesterton, *Saint Thomas Aquinas* (New York: Doubleday, 1956), 141.

a fool. All I could do was cling in faith to the word the Lord had planted so clearly in my heart.

And then, the miracle happened, and the fool became a prophet. I have added Richard's story to the story of Nneka's faith, in order to inspire you to believe with me for a fresh revival in America. I want you to believe that God has indeed spoken, saying, *America will be saved.* When your faith rises with mine, we will see a mighty wave of revival sweep across this land, similar to the one I have already witnessed in Africa.

I pray that this book will have a special role in leading multitudes to Christ. This is my goal in writing it. May the Holy Spirit quicken the truth of the gospel to your heart as you read it.

DAY OF DECISION

1

DAY OF DECISION

For more than a decade, Daniel's story has been told. He has distilled his story into a single document and has spoken to audiences around the world. As with all stories, each storyteller approaches the events of their tale from a unique angle. Each one brings out details that others might have missed or considered unimportant. It is similar to the Gospels: Matthew, Mark, Luke, and John. Taken together, these four books provide a broader, more complete picture of Jesus' life than any one version would have done by itself.

With that in mind, this is the first version of Daniel's story told from my own unique—and until now—unexplained part in this drama.

Before I begin, I ask you to put yourself in my shoes on Saturday, December 1, 2001—twenty-four hours before the miracle happened.

You will find me in my room at the Sheraton Hotel in Lagos, Nigeria. Do you remember where you were on that day? Do you remember what was on your mind? I do. I will never forget it. These were world-changing times for me, and I had on my heart a big burden to pray.

A NO-BRAINER

This burden to pray resulted from several issues that had been pressing on me. Primarily, it came from a major decision I faced—the question of whether I should move my family and ministry from Frankfurt, Germany, to Orlando, Florida. At the time, my team was producing a motion-picture series in Orlando entitled Full Flame. It was an eight-episode documentary drawn from my life experiences. We were also publishing study guides that would supplement the content of each film and teach our outreach methods to young evangelists around the world.

This project was to be a legacy of my ministry, and it was a huge undertaking. It meant that I had to travel again and again to Universal Studios in Florida to film the documentary segments. My team suggested that if I moved there, it would save hundreds of hours of travel time, reduce the wear and tear on my body, and give me more time to spend at home with my family. Not to mention, it would also save us hundreds of thousands of dollars in production costs. It was, as they say, a "no-brainer." It made perfect business sense. Yet I could not make the decision so easily.

It was not perfect business sense that had led my evangelistic ministry, Christ for All Nations, to the kind of success we had been experiencing. In fact, the Spirit of God had led us to a harvest no other evangelist had ever witnessed in the recorded history of the church. Who was I to impose mere business sense on the work of the Lord? I had offices in the United Kingdom, Canada, Australia, Hong Kong, Singapore, Nigeria, and South Africa. However, the executive and management decisions proceeded from Frankfurt, Germany, where I lived. Germany was my fatherland, by birth and by divine guidance. God had ordained it to be so.

For those who do not know me, let me pause to introduce myself.

I am Reinhard Bonnke, a German-born evangelist. I went to South Africa in 1967 as a missionary. That move was not undertaken lightly. I had received a clear call to Africa as ten-year-old boy. I was the son of a German Pentecostal preacher, but not even my parents believed in my call. Shortly after my arrival in Africa at the age of twenty-seven, the Lord moved me away from the status of "missionary."

The mission organization had kept me preaching primarily to white people. In 1968, I began to preach to black people, and I experienced the true passion of my calling. I began playing my accordion to attract crowds on the streets of Maseru, in the mountain kingdom of Lesotho. Sometimes, I preached only to the two or three people who had stopped to stare at the blond-haired, blue-eyed foreigner playing and singing in a language they did not understand. The small size of my crowds did not affect me. I preached the same then as I do now, through an interpreter; except that today, the crowds can number more than one million people. But no one begins at the top. After becoming an evangelist in 1968, I began to reach more and more Africans as I followed the still, small voice of the Spirit of God within my heart. (See 1 Kings 19:12.)

In 1986, after eighteen years in South Africa, the Lord directed me to move my headquarters to Frankfurt. I was forty-six years old. The divine timing of this move prevented the stain of apartheid from affecting the work of our ministry. For the next eight years, South Africa struggled to transition to its new form of democracy. Meanwhile, Christ for All Nations was catapulted into favor and prominence all over Africa. This was not the kind of blessing that came from careful business planning. It had come from the hand of God alone, and I knew it.

Then, in 2000, we experienced the Millennium Crusade in Lagos, Nigeria. It marked a pinnacle in the journey of that young German boy who had heard the voice of God calling him to Africa to win souls for Christ. On the final night of that crusade, I preached the gospel to a crowd of 1.6 million people. My team had trained more than 200,000 people to follow up with the attendees over the course of six days of meetings. Those workers were equipped with $1.2 million in books and discipleship materials. We had 2,000 ushers and 1,000 local policemen for crowd control. On that final night, when I gave the invitation for sinners to repent, 1,093,000 people made the decision to put their faith in Jesus. Over those six days, more than 6 million Nigerians attended the crusade, with a total of 3,461,171 decisions for Christ registered. These numbers stagger the mind.

PRESERVING THE MILLENNIUM HARVEST

On Saturday, December 1, 2001, as I pondered the question of whether to move to America, we were still riding the crest of the Millennium Crusade. I had recently traveled the one hundred miles from Ibadan to Lagos, in order to rest and prepare for the final meetings of the year in the smaller city of Oshogbo, Nigeria. In Ibadan, our crowds had swelled to 1.3 million people by the final night. A total of 3.9 million people had attended the event, with more than 2.6 million accepting Christ.

The supernatural millennium harvest was continuing at full force in 2001. This is called *momentum.* Anyone who watches sporting events knows the power of momentum. An inferior team can often defeat a superior team by riding a wave of momentum to an unexpected result. With such momentum moving our ministry, how could I risk stopping it by undertaking such a drastic change of relocating to a different continent? We had registered more than 52 million decisions for Christ during more than a decade of directing our efforts from our home in Frankfurt.

Adding to the pressure, the upcoming meetings in Oshogbo were heavy on my mind. I had recently received a phone call telling me that Sunday Aranziola, the young bass guitarist scheduled to play in our crusade band, had been martyred in Oshogbo by Muslim extremists only a few days prior. This killing had occurred only two months after the September 11 attacks in the U.S. The whole world was reeling with fear and uncertainty. How many worshippers of Allah would be stirred to strike a blow for the cause of jihad? Nobody knew. This young man named Sunday had been targeted while putting up Reinhard Bonnke crusade posters throughout the city. The radicals had followed him to his home, waited for the cover of darkness, and then had broken down the door and, in front of his father and mother, dragged him from his bed, beating him with clubs.

"Jesus, what shall I do?" his father had heard him call as he was driven from the house into the darkened street. "What shall I do?"

"Say 'Allahu akbar'!" the young men demanded. "Say it! 'Allahu akbar'!"

This is an Islamic phrase, meaning "God is greatest."

"Jesus is Lord!" Sunday replied.

Those were his last words before they beat him to death.

Christians in Oshogbo were enraged. They threatened to retaliate with violence against the Muslim population. Oshogbo was home to the Grand Mosque, located at the center of the city. The situation was as dangerous as a candle burning in a pool of gasoline. My team had cleared a large field on the edge of the city, far from the mosque. Oshogbo had a soccer stadium near the city center that seated ten thousand people, but we had rejected it. Even if we had filled the playing field and the stands to standing room only, it would have accommodated only a fraction of the crowds of people who had been attending our crusades in Nigeria. Such a crowd, if aroused to violence, would have jeopardized all the momentum of the supernatural harvest we had just experienced in Nigeria. This very thing had happened before.

Ever in my memory was the crusade of October 1991, in Kano, Nigeria. Our coming to the city had sparked violence from the Muslims living there, as well. Our team had been forced to flee the city, seeing dead bodies and wreckage in the streets as they fled. Muslim mobs ruled the day, and Christians were being killed on sight. Hundreds died.

The rumor mill blamed us for that mayhem. For most people, alas, perception is reality. They believed what they read in the newspapers, and the word-of-mouth gossip spread. "Bonnke brought violence to Kano;

how can he claim to serve the Prince of Peace?" Our supposed culpability became our reputation, even though an extensive investigation was conducted, after which the local governor issued a report exonerating us of all blame. Nevertheless, Christ for All Nations was banned from Nigeria for nearly a decade. At the time, it appeared that Satan had won the day and that Jesus had been forced to retreat.

Through an incredible journey of faith and miracles, all of which are documented in my autobiography, *Living a Life of Fire*, we had been invited back into the country in 1999. The explosion of positive response at our return was beyond anything that could have been planned or anticipated. What Satan had meant for evil, God turned into an absolutely unprecedented harvest. The crusades we held in 2000, and those that followed in 2001, made us a household name in this nation of 140 million souls.

SINCERELY, OSAMA BIN LADEN

Once again, in Oshogbo, the specter of violence raised its ugly head. At first, I prepared our team to cancel the meetings and put our equipment into storage until the following season. Then we received a message from the Muslim governor of Osun State. He had been privy to the extensive study of the violence in Kano and knew that we were not to blame.

"If anyone can bring peace to Oshogbo and prevent an outbreak of religious war, it is Reinhard Bonnke," he said.

He believed that cancelling the meetings was more likely to trigger violence than my coming and preaching to the crowds, due to the disappointment that would result. He knew that our message was one of life and not death, and he urged my team not to cancel. After considering his request with great care, we agreed to go forward. But we had no guarantee of success. Nor could we offer a guarantee that peace would rule the day. That remained beyond our control.

So much was happening of such magnitude, I could not sort it out in the natural.

Six months before the September 11 attacks, I had received a threatening personal message from none other than Osama bin Laden. The same message was sent to all of our offices around the world. I had been put on Al-Qaeda's hit list because I had dared to lead Muslims to faith in Jesus Christ at an Easter crusade in Khartoum, Sudan, earlier that year. Moreover, I was mindful of the fact that several of the Al-Qaeda terrorists who had piloted planes into the buildings on September 11, 2001, had trained just miles from my would-be home in Florida. A move to America would hardly keep me out of the crosshairs. To put it mildly, this was no ordinary day of decision in my life and ministry.

I have tried to give you a glimpse of my situation on Saturday, December 1, 2001, in Lagos, Nigeria. I cannot imagine how anyone could have stood in my shoes and faced such choices without trembling. Actually, I was not standing; I was moving back and forth like a caged lion. I had set aside the entire day for prayer—prayer, fasting, and pacing. Lots of pacing. In my autobiography, I wrote about that day:

> I paced so much I nearly wore out the carpet. "Lord, should I make the move to Orlando? Yes or no? What is Your direction to me?" Finally, in the afternoon, I reached a place of peace.

This hardly tells the whole story. I left out critical details that I now share with you. You see, when I wrote my autobiography, I deliberately left out Daniel's story, because I always believed that it deserved a book of its own.

PEACE AND REST

As I paced and prayed, I sought a moment when peace would flood my soul. Whenever I am faced with a difficult decision, I seek to have the peace of God rule in my heart. This is a spiritual peace that bypasses the mind. The apostle Paul described it in Scripture as the peace *"which passeth all understanding"* (Philippians 4:7). As I prayed, I received that peace in the late afternoon. How can I describe it? Nothing in my circumstances had changed. I can tell you only that I stopped pacing, I stopped praying, and I stopped fasting. It is important to know, however, that this peace did not come from knowing the best decision to make. It came from knowing that God had heard my prayer and had answered it. He had not made the answer known to my mind, but He had downloaded His peace into my spirit.

We are creatures with a body, soul, and spirit. Our soul is where the mind lives. When we receive an answer from the Holy Spirit, peace in our spirit is the result. But it is a peace that passes understanding. That means the mind is not the channel for it. This is where the mind must operate in faith, believing what the Spirit has spoken, in spite of any natural evidence to the contrary.

The apostle Paul provided our best descriptions of this kind of faith. He said, "*For we walk by faith, not by sight*" (2 Corinthians 5:7). In another place, he said, "*For now we see through a glass, darkly...*" (1 Corinthians 13:12). Just before that, he wrote, "*We know in part, and we prophesy in part*" (1 Corinthians 13:9). It is important to trust the Word of God above our own thoughts and feelings in all matters. This is especially true in difficult decisions. That day, everything I saw with my eyes, and everything I understood with my mind, would have led me in a very different direction from that of the peace in my heart. And so, I had peace but no clear answer.

Facing the circumstances of that day, I decided to do something I had never done before. While I do not recommend it as a regular practice, there are no pat formulas with God; He does not dance to our tune. But we are in a relationship with Him—a relationship as unique and as individual as our DNA, our fingerprints, and our retinal scans.

I think of the relationship the Savior had with Peter and John, recorded in John's gospel. This relationship was illustrated well in the account of the Last Supper, when Jesus told Peter that his life would end in martyrdom. Peter was naturally not happy to hear it. Who would welcome such news? He turned and saw John, who had laid his head on Jesus' chest. John seemed to seek a relationship with Jesus in a way Peter never would have considered. Peter wondered if Jesus would give John special treatment because of his tender, affectionate nature. He wondered if *"the other disciple, whom Jesus loved"* (John 20:2) would escape the kind of martyrdom that he faced.

> *Peter seeing him saith to Jesus, Lord, and what shall this man do? Jesus saith unto him, If I will that he tarry till I come, what is that to thee? follow thou me.* (John 21:21–22)

Each of us receives our own answer. Our relationship with Jesus is not determined by someone else's relationship with Him. It is one-to-one, and He delights in our childlike trust. *"Ask, and it shall be given you,"* He said; *"seek, and ye shall find"* (Matthew 7:7).

In a moment of bold inspiration, I asked God—who had first called me as a child—for a sign that would now confirm that I should go ahead with the move to America. In essence, I put a kind of "fleece" before the Lord, as Gideon did. (See Judges 6:36–40.) Oh, I know there are those who will now criticize me for this Old Testament method of hearing from God. I humbly suggest that the Lord might answer, as He did to Peter, *"What is that to thee?"* Each of us must follow Him in the integrity of our heart.

THE ULTIMATE SIGN

For those who do not know what is meant by a "fleece," let me describe it to you. In the sixth chapter of the book of Judges, Gideon took the fleece of a lamb and placed it on the ground as night fell. He wanted to be sure that God would be with him in the coming battle against an army of overwhelming odds, and so he asked that in the morning, he would find the fleece drenched with dew, yet the ground around it dry, if God was going to deliver the enemy into his hand. The next morning, the fleece was indeed wet—Gideon wrung a bowlful of dew from it, in fact—while the ground was dry. But, like us, Gideon still saw through a darkened glass. He knew in part, but his mind was still beset by uncertainty. *Perhaps*, he suspected, *the ground was naturally saturated with the dew, while the fleece naturally retained the moisture.* In other words, he suspected that nature had spoken, not God. So, he begged God to allow him to ask for one more sign. He asked that the next morning, the fleece would be dry, while the ground around it was wet. And so it was. God did not reject or despise Gideon for seeking this extra measure of reassurance.

In my case, in that hotel room in Lagos, I asked for something very specific. I said, "Lord, I am asking You for a sign. I've never asked You for signs, but this time, I need a sign. If You want me to move to America, I want You to do something that I have never ever seen happen in my ministry."

Now, the Lord knew I had seen thousands of amazing miracles. When the gospel is preached, blind eyes are opened, cripples leap and walk, the deaf hear, and the mute speak. Doors even open to prisoners on death row. In this case, however, something spectacular would have to occur that would rise above all of those past miracles. It never entered my mind to wonder what it would be. Little did I know, as I asked for a sign in that hotel room in Lagos, that Daniel Ekechukwu was lying dead in a coffin in the Ikeduru General Hospital mortuary, partially embalmed with formaldehyde, and that, in less than twenty-four hours, our paths would cross, and he would rise from the dead.

In total ignorance of such matters, I went to dinner at the hotel eatery, the Crockpot Restaurant. Then, after preparing myself for Sunday, I went to bed.

"HE'S BREATHING!"

2

"HE'S BREATHING!"

Sunday morning, December 2, 2001, began with a ride to the airport. A charter plane was waiting on the tarmac to fly me to Onitsha, where I was to preach at the dedication of Grace Cathedral, a ten-thousand-seat church newly built by Pastor Paul C. NwaChukwu. It is rare that I agree to participate in the dedication of a church building. My policy has been to say no. Once I start down the road of accepting such invitations, there will be a flood of requests, and not enough of me to go around.

In this case, I made an exception. I felt a special bond with Pastor Paul because of the crusade meetings we had held in Onitsha six months earlier. He had been a prime force in organizing the cooperation of local churches and pastors there. When we hold an outreach in a city, we schedule meetings with local churches, pastors, and believers in something we call a Fire Conference. We train them in time-tested methods of evangelism. We show them how to document and later follow up with those who make a decision to accept Christ as Savior during the campaign. Through the Fire Conference, we connect new converts with local believers who can disciple them after we leave. We also inspire the local believers to become evangelists who are bold in their witness, leading others into a relationship with the Father. The Fire Conference is the heart and soul of our outreach efforts.

In the spring of 2001, we held the Onitsha Fire Conference and outreach campaign. Onitsha is a city of little more than one million people, but we had 800,000 in attendance in a single service during the crusade meetings there. This meant that we needed our Fire Conference follow-up trainees more than ever.

Beyond that, an amazing record had been set here—not in attendance in responses. An astonishing 86 percent of those who attended the Onitsha meetings responded to the call for salvation. Never in all my life had I seen such rich soil for the gospel. Never in my crusades had I witnessed a higher percentage of sinners coming to Jesus. This is a thrill perhaps equal to that of preaching to 1.6 million people in Lagos in 2000. An evangelist lives for the day when *everyone* in his audience is without Christ. He longs for the meeting in which *all* who hear the gospel receive Christ. I have seen such things in my dreams, but in Onitsha, I came close to realizing it. Eighty-six percent received Jesus. Hallelujah!

Pastor Paul Nwachukwu had promised me that at the dedication of Grace Cathedral, a local team of nearly one thousand young evangelists would be present. They had been members of his congregation, recruited as a result of our Fire Conference training. I would be invited to lay hands on them and pray for an impartation of the spirit of evangelism into their lives. What an incentive. Not only would I be cutting the ribbon for a structure of bricks and mortar, but also—even better—I would be ministering to flesh-and-blood men and women who were burning with the same zeal that I knew. Nothing could have pleased me more than to see the fruit of our harvest in Onitsha multiply through the lives of these soulwinners. For all of these reasons, Pastor Paul had remained dear to my heart, and I made an exception to my policy of not attending church dedications.

WISE AS A SERPENT

I agreed to come to Onitsha under one condition: immediately afterward, I would be flown to Oshogbo, where Sunday Aranziola had died. Events there were of utmost importance. The Muslim governor of Osun State had sent me a special invitation to meet with him, and I was anxious to do so. I wanted to learn the reasons for his belief that our meetings would avert bloodshed. In such face-to-face encounters with political leaders, I am able to assert that Christ is the King of Kings, Lord of Lords, and Prince of Peace. They hear from me that the name of Jesus is the only name under heaven by which we must be saved. (See Acts 4:12.) Whether the leader is Muslim, Hindu, animist, or atheist, my message does not vary.

I also knew that, as governor, this man was privy to a great deal of information from police and other sources about the situation in Oshogbo. Our team wanted to be informed so that we could cooperate with the authorities in every possible way. In addition, I would invite the governor to join me on the platform at our meetings. If he was amenable, I would have him make public remarks to the people. I believed that a demonstration of solidarity between the Muslim governor and myself would help calm the waters, still turbulent in the wake of the murder of Sunday Aranziola.

After meeting with the governor, I planned to meet with Sunday's grieving parents. I wanted to share their pain and tears. I wanted to tell them of my great admiration for their son. I felt completely humbled and sobered by the full measure of his sacrifice for Jesus. I believed that a great harvest in Oshogbo was ready to spring up from the seed of his martyrdom, and I wanted to share that promise with them.

HARMLESS AS A DOVE

As I boarded my flight for Onitsha, I was told about a host of news reporters gathering in Oshogbo to meet me. I was not sure what to do about them. In the aftermath of 9/11, news of Sunday's death had caught the attention of the major news organizations in Europe, as well as Nigeria. Now they were flocking to Oshogbo, hoping to arrive in advance of any bloodshed so they could exploit it in the press. I was told that reporters were seeking to interview me. I am not flattered by such attention. I do not often grant interviews, knowing that many reporters are only marginally interested in the truth. Most are seeking sensational headlines that will discredit our ministry back home. I had made no prior agreements with them, and I decided that I would address media requests on a case-by-case basis. I would cooperate only if their intentions seemed honorable, and then only if my ministry schedule would allow it.

Upon landing in Onitsha, I was met by deacons from the church and by government security forces carrying AK-47 rifles. The security chief approached me and said he was under orders from President Olusegun Obasanjo to see that no harm came my way while I was in Onitsha. He assured me that he had men at the church who were carefully screening the crowd of people who had gathered for the dedication. As I entered the car the church had provided for me, the security men entered vans and mounted motorcycles. Our escorted motorcade then made its way from the airport to the church.

The potential for Christian and Muslim violence wherever I went was of great concern to Nigeria's political leaders in 2001. The rulers, from President Obasanjo on down, had pledged to protect me. I found security forces waiting to escort me at every stop. Some of these measures were, of course, merely for the sake of practicality. The elected officials had never seen crowds nearly as large as those drawn by a Christ for All Nations crusade. These crowds represented a bloc of voters they did not wish to offend. In that regard, they were determined not to see a repeat of the violence in Kano.

In this, I was merely grateful for their concern. I steered clear of endorsing any politician or political party, except to publicly thank all of the authorities for their efforts to promote a peaceful meeting. As for President Obasanjo, I had ministered to him in private, years before he came to power. One of the first acts of his new administration in 1999 was to lift the ban on Christ for All Nations in Nigeria. He had been primarily responsible for our return there.

A PLACE CALLED GRACE

After negotiating the obstacle course that is a Nigerian road, our motorcade arrived at Grace Cathedral. The church building was filled to overflowing. As we drew nearer, we could hear the sounds of worship being projected by loudspeakers mounted on the building's exterior. The very ground seemed to shake. Perched on a hilltop, the building appeared massive, nearly square and about four stories tall. The three main floors were accessible from ground level at the front of the building. In the back, there were offices and classrooms above a full walkout basement, where the hillside descended to a lower level.

The red clay soil all around had been graded to create parking areas. As is the case throughout much of Africa, no asphalt was evident. My vehicle was driven through the milling crowds to a private entrance on the main level. Security officers guarded the entrance as I was ushered through the door and into the pastor's study. Other security forces were deployed around the perimeter, joining the earlier force that had patted down and screened everyone entering the building.

Once inside, I embraced Pastor Paul and his wife, Dorothy, who welcomed me and led me to a seat. A row of overstuffed chairs had been placed at the front of the platform for pastors and special guests. I was offered a seat of honor next to Paul and Dorothy. The pastoral team and elders, together with a large choir, were seated behind me on risers. Looking out at the crowd, I could see that the front rows were occupied by guests in armless plastic chairs—the kind that allow more bodies to be crowded together in a single row. A dozen rows back, all seating had been abandoned. It was standing room only. I assumed that the local fire marshal was present, because those standing had been arranged in well-defined aisles, free of all obstructions. It was as if their feet had been bolted to the floor.

We had used such methods in our Christ for All Nations crusade meetings, as well. Long ago, we had abandoned any hope of seating so many people. Instead of looking to stadiums to hold our crowds, we used bulldozers to clear a natural amphitheatre from a hillside, large enough for the crowd to stand shoulder to shoulder and still have an unobstructed line of sight to the podium and clear aisles in case of an emergency. These folks stood for hours—before, during, and after a crusade meeting, come rain or shine, wind or lightning. The hunger for God in Africa is such that no one thinks twice about comfort. The people who had gathered in Grace Cathedral that morning were typical of so many I had seen elsewhere.

As I took my seat, the worship team was leading the congregation in singing traditional African music, accompanied by dancing and clapping. African worship is enthusiastic and energetic, and I greatly appreciate it. Of course, when I speak to Africans, I am equally enthusiastic and energetic. Perhaps that is one reason I connect so well with audiences in this great land.

The atmosphere at Grace Cathedral was absolutely electric. You could not be heard by the person next to you unless you shouted. With pleasure, I noticed that the balcony balusters around the room had been decorated with banners bearing the slogan from our Fire Conferences: "A Fire for Every Head." We teach that on the day of Pentecost, tongues of fire came down on the head of every person in the upper room in Jerusalem. (See Acts 2:3.) This symbol from heaven told the truth. Although there were 120 in that upper room, the Holy Spirit made Himself completely available to each person, individually. I was glad to see that this idea had taken root here at Grace Cathedral.

The speaking platform was arranged partially in the round, extending into the room. Thousands sat and stood before me on the main floor, with thousands more crowded into the second-level balcony, which wrapped around us in a U shape. Seeing so many in the balcony, I secretly prayed that Pastor Paul had hired adequate structural engineers for the construction of this auditorium, for we were surely testing the weight limits.

WIND OF THE SPIRIT

The order of service took us through the musical preliminaries to the announcements and finally to the dedication ceremony. I cut the ribbon and offered a prayer of dedication for Grace Cathedral, a lighthouse of hope anchored in the red soil of Onitsha, Anambra State. Next on the program was the presentation of evangelists—nearly one thousand of them, each with the flame of the Holy Spirit burning on his or her head. They stood and crowded the platform. Pastor Paul announced that he and his leadership team had named this outreach "Kingdom Life World Evangelism." The name inspired me. Grace Cathedral in Onitsha was not just looking at its own backyard for spreading the gospel. They were taking the Great Commission seriously by going into all the world. I love an evangelistic vision of unlimited view. The walls of every local church must include the ends of the earth.

As I stood to pray for these young men and women, the wind of the Holy Spirit seemed to hit me. As often happens in these circumstances, unplanned words came from my mouth. "Today," I said, "something is going to happen at Grace Cathedral that will shake the ends of the earth— something that will make the ears of those who hear it tingle everywhere!" These words were recorded that day. They have been replayed, again and again, in the years since, because of the event that soon followed.

I prayed and placed my hands on as many as I could before I began to preach. The message the Lord impressed me to deliver was "The River of God." There is a river that flows from the Spirit of God, and it is unlimited in power and potential. Yet so many sit on the banks of the river, merely enjoying picnics. Others wade in the shallows, content to splash around in water up to their ankles. I challenged the people to dive in and swim in the river of God—to let its power sweep them to the ends of the earth with the message of His salvation.

They tell me it was somewhere around one in the afternoon when we heard a commotion outside the building. Ignoring it, I continued to preach. In Africa, commotions are not unusual. If I always allowed myself to be distracted by such noise, I suppose I would never finish a sermon. I pressed on to the end of the sermon, and then we ministered to those whose hearts had been touched. I sensed that many lives would never be the same after that day. It was glorious.

Afterward, many people remained in the sanctuary to continue seeking God in prayer. Meanwhile, Pastor Paul and my Africa director, John Darku, escorted me to the pastor's study. We shut the door. Our plan was to get into the car as soon as possible and return to the airport. But first, as we normally do, we discussed the meeting and how the people had responded.

It is always necessary for me to take some time to unwind after preaching a sermon. During this time, I have enthusiasm. I feel the wind of the Spirit. I sense that I have been used to touch the hearts of people, and there is nothing on earth like that feeling. It is my food and drink—my very life itself.

After we had settled a bit, we prepared to exit to the motorcade and return to the airport. It was then that Pastor Paul presented me with a gift to thank me for coming to his dedication service. It was a fine wristwatch. In light of the events of that day, I call it my "resurrection watch." After presenting the watch, Pastor Paul left the room to confer with one of his staff members, who had urgently requested his presence back in the sanctuary.

DIVINE DISTURBANCE

Suddenly there came a loud banging on the opposite door. It was the door that led to the rear section of the building, where the offices were housed, and it was secured on the outside with heavy locks. The knocking was so loud and forceful, John Darku grew fearful. He thought that perhaps thieves had broken through the security forces and had come to rob us.

I went to the door and demanded, "Who is there? What do you want?"

"He's breathing! He's breathing! He's breathing!"

"What do you mean, 'he's breathing'? We all breathe. Who is breathing?"

"He's breathing."

The commotion died down, but I could hear excited voices outside, as people crowded into the hallway. I decided not to unlock the door unless Pastor Paul returned and decided to do it. Outside the door, a certain amount of chaos was in motion. Crowd control under such circumstances is a serious matter.

Pastor Paul returned. "The story is that a woman brought the corpse of her husband into the basement of the church," he explained. "She believed he would be raised from the dead, if only she could bring him here where you were preaching. He was dead for three days. They say now he is breathing."

I was nearly dumbstruck. "That's what they were saying—'he's breathing.' I should see this for myself."

"No, please," Pastor Paul insisted. "The crowd is flooding into the basement. They are running here from surrounding neighborhoods. The word is spreading like wildfire. They say Bonnke's anointing has brought this to pass. They believe the anointing remains in the clothes you wear, and they would tear them to pieces just to have a thread of them."

"But I did nothing. I did not even pray for the man."

"Yes, I know. But you should get into the car now. I will quickly check on things in the sanctuary and give you a report. I dare not go into the basement. But if you don't leave now, you might not get to Oshogbo."

"Very well," I said.

John and I went out the door, and the security officers opened the doors to our car and then shut us inside. We could see crowds of excited people running toward the building. Others began to crowd around our car, but the security officers kept them away. Soon, Pastor Paul came out and joined us, and our driver quickly moved away from the building, along with the other vehicles.

"The dead man's father is in the sanctuary," said Pastor Paul. "He stood up and said to me, 'It is true. My son was dead and is now breathing.' But he said, 'His body is still as stiff as iron.' My staff is with the man in the basement, and they will keep a close watch on this situation. I will sort it out when I come back."

"Something surely happened here," I said. "But was it a hoax, or real?"

Paul replied, "Exactly."

As we drove away, I used my satellite cell phone and dialed the number of Robert Murphree, our film producer from Orlando. He had come with us to Nigeria and was preparing to interview people who had experienced miracles in our past crusades. I told him about what had just happened in Onitsha. "I think this is too important to ignore," I said. "You should come here and bring your camera crew, now. Investigate this story and report back to me. If it is not rock solid, then we will let it go. But if it is true, then the most outstanding miracle I have ever known just took place."

Robert replied, "I have scheduled other interviews. How soon do you want me to come?"

"Immediately," I said. "The people are still here at Grace Cathedral as we speak. We should not let them disappear. Come meet with Pastor Paul's staff. They will connect you to this story. I will go on to Oshogbo, and then I will get your full report when you have had some time to check it out. Take as much time as you need."

We arrived at the airport, and as we walked toward the airplane, the police chief in charge of our security approached me. That morning, when we had first met on the tarmac, he had appeared to be strong and self-assured. Now, he looked disturbed. He was trembling, and his voice shook as he spoke. "Pastor Bonnke?"

"Yes? What can I do for you?"

"Sir, I am a Muslim. I have never seen such a thing. When they brought the corpse to the church, it was in a coffin. I made them take the body out of the coffin so that I could inspect it for explosives. The body was stiff with rigor mortis. I pulled wads of cotton out of the man's nostrils. They took him into the basement, and now he is breathing. Pastor Bonnke, I've seen him. The man who was dead is breathing."

This Muslim policeman removed his dark glasses and looked at me with wonder in his eyes. What he had seen had rocked him to the core. Surely, his view of Jesus as a mere prophet had been changed forever. We declare Christ to be the very Son of God, and here was a sign to confirm that message. Looking at him, it began to dawn on me that this thing had really happened. My television crew was about to record the story of their lives.

RECEIVING THE SIGN

On the tarmac, I called my wife, Anni, in Frankfurt. "Anni," I said, "begin immediately to prepare our house for a move to Florida."

"Oh, no," she said. "Did you forget? Our children are planning to come from America to Frankfurt to celebrate Christmas with us."

"I did not forget. Tell them to cancel the airline tickets. This year we will celebrate Christmas in our new home in Orlando."

The next morning, newspaper headlines across Nigeria read "Bonnke Raises Man from the Dead!" This was not true. I had not even been aware of the incident until after the fact. But no amount of correction could stop the news media's lust for tabloid sensationalism. I believe God used the publicity to fuel the atmosphere of our meetings in Oshogbo. The crusade would now be conducted under a banner of fame for both a murder and a resurrection. Incredible! I suppose the best public relations team on the planet would have had to bow to the effect of this news on our meetings. No one planned it. No one foresaw it. No one could take glory for it. People began to surge toward the city from great distances to be in place the next time I was scheduled to stand on a platform and preach.

The 2001 Oshogbo campaign became a tremendous year-end effort for us in Nigeria. The terrorism of the Muslim radicals failed. The news of Sunday Aranziola's last words rocked not just the city but the entire state. The Muslim governor expressed his condolences and proclaimed public solidarity for our meetings, and many Muslims openly attended to hear the preaching. On stage, we celebrated Sunday's life and mourned his death with family and friends. The crowds grew to double the size of the city of Oshogbo, having drawn people from the entire region.

During the meetings, a Swiss journalist writing for *SonntagsZeitung*, a Zurich newspaper, reported that the closest hotel room he could find was thirty miles from our meeting site. All available lodging was occupied by people attending the meetings. He reported that he had hired a local Muslim driver to guide him through the teeming crowds at the crusade grounds. Apparently, this Swiss man had never experienced the gospel preached to the masses with conviction and power. He had come from a European culture steeped in dead religion.

It was amusing to read how he described the meeting in terms that his audience would understand. He quoted Karl Marx's famous assertion, "Religion is the opiate of the people." What Marx meant, of course, is that religion gives ignorant people a false sense of happiness, as opium does. As we know, Marxist Communists have tried for nearly a century to wipe Christianity out of existence, with no success. Having mingled with the enthusiastic seekers in our meeting, this reporter wrote, "If it is true that religion is the opiate of the people, then Bonnke serves the purest heroin."

He delivered an insult and a compliment at the same time. I accepted the compliment. I knew he was overwhelmed and unable to understand the wind of the Spirit that blows through crowds of people coming to know Jesus as their Savior. In his experience, heroin was the only thing he knew to be as powerful as the effect of our preaching. He lacked a proper framework to explain it.

Later in his article, he described the effect the sermon had on his Muslim driver and guide. I, of course, remember it from my position on the platform. I preached a familiar message. It was a sermon based on the idea that saying no to Jesus is to deny the salvation God has made available through His name. And so, at a certain point in the sermon, I invited the crowd to interact with me by shouting "Yes to Jesus!"

The reporter wrote that as the crowd responded, there was a deafening roar: "Yes to Jesus!" He looked to the side and saw that his Muslim driver was totally swept up in the moment. He had forgotten himself and had become some kind of Christian on the spot. His hands were raised to the heavens, and he cried at the top of his voice, "I say yes to Jesus! Yes to Jesus! Yes to Jesus!" The reporter was so rattled by the experience that when he returned to his hotel room in the wee hours of the morning, he could not sleep. For the rest of the night, he reported, the roar of the crowd echoed in his ears: *Yes to Jesus! Yes to Jesus! Yes to Jesus!*"

I am quite proud of having given that reporter a sleepless night. However, it is my sincere prayer that, at some point, he took the message to heart and said "yes to Jesus" for himself. By the final night of the Oshogbo crusade, we counted 650,000 in attendance at a single meeting, nearly double the population of the city. Through five nights of preaching, more than 1.5 million decisions for Christ were registered. Indeed, a great harvest did spring from the seed of Sunday's martyrdom.

After the crusade, I prepared to return to Frankfurt to begin the moving process. Before leaving Nigeria, however, I could hardly contain my excitement about the miracle in Onitsha. I again called my television producer, Robert Murphree.

"Robert, what is happening? Give me your report. Is the miracle true?"

"Reinhard, it is true. We are filming as we speak."

"Is it verifiable?"

"From many sources."

"Tell me then, Robert. Tell me everything. What happened in Onitsha?"

HEARTS REVEALED

3

HEARTS REVEALED

As our television production team investigated the wonderful story of Daniel Ekechukwu's resurrection, they found that the miracle was well documented from many surprising sources. They retraced the route Daniel's body had traveled to Grace Cathedral in Onitsha, this time guided by Daniel himself, alive and well. What a stunning trip! In the process, they captured video of some mind-blowing moments that verified the resurrection beyond a reasonable doubt. These scenes are available for you to see in the companion documentary to this book, also titled *Raised from the Dead*.

The effect of the video interviews was nearly overwhelming to the crew. They felt as if they had been dumped into a "twilight zone," where none of their normal perceptions was relevant. The sights, smells, foods, and customs of Nigeria mingled with the story like foreign incense as they worked. They were in a kind of culture shock, experiencing the wonder of this resurrection on top of the unfamiliar cross section of African life. The experience would not allow them to shut down easily at day's end, and they told me they did not sleep well.

At the same time, a few unsettling details emerged. First, and perhaps most puzzling, was that this miracle began with a scene of domestic violence. On the Thursday prior, there had been an incident of physical abuse between Daniel and his wife, Nneka. This occurred little more than twenty-four hours before he died. The couple was embarrassed but did not shy away from discussing it, when asked. To them, the incident was central to the entire sequence of events that followed.

I can almost sense the thoughts in your head. Thoughts like, *Throw this book in the trash. God would never raise a man from the dead after he had struck his wife.* Well, I hate to have to tell you this, but it was even worse than that. At the very beginning of this miracle story, we find a messy detail most of us would choose to sweep under the rug, to be left out of the story altogether. It simply does not fit with our preconceived notions of the circumstances in which God might raise someone from the dead. And that is the very reason I think we should take a look at it.

The truth is, I, too, would rather omit this detail from the story. I have always been uncomfortable with it. And I might have ignored it, except that Daniel and his wife have shared it, again and again. As time has passed, I have thought more about it, and I now realize that it is a detail of God's choosing, not my own. There is divine gold in this picture of human failure.

WOUNDED HEARTS

Before proceeding, however, we should clear up the misconception that men are the only perpetrators of domestic violence. While it is statistically true that among married couples, men exhibit violence more often than women. in this case, Daniel did not strike his wife. She struck him.

Once again, I sense thoughts such as, *Well, if she struck him, he certainly must have done something to deserve it!* I have to chuckle, because only God would choose to demonstrate His resurrection power in such a volatile circumstance. There is simply no politically correct way to deal with it.

But it seems to me that the very circumstance itself reveals more than the failings of Daniel and Nneka. It uncovers pride and prejudice deeply rooted in our own thinking. As we feel the urge to reject this couple and their entire story because of this detail, we demand that God dance to our tune. But if this miracle indeed took place, then we must deal with the fact that it did not happen under circumstances of which we would approve. But God's ways are high above ours, and I begin to see where this story is leading. No one is going to be left untouched by the love, mercy, and grace of God—not even a couple deep in marital trouble.

By this messy detail, we are pushed out of our comfort zones. But we are also pushed to examine our own hearts. And so should we, because God's love comes alive only for those who have been made aware of their utter need for Him. Scripture tells us that Jesus did not come to seek the righteous but to save sinners. (See Mark 2:17; Luke 5:32.) We had not repented, had not yet asked for forgiveness, had not reformed our behavior; and yet, while we were still in our sins, He died for us and removed the penalty we deserved. He came as the Good Shepherd, the One who left the flock to find the one lost sheep.

In the Gospels, we read that Jesus was criticized for spending time with people who did not even pretend to be religious. Some were notorious sinners, like the scandalous woman who washed His feet with her tears and dried them with her hair in the home of a self-righteous Pharisee. In these biblical scenes, again and again, the love of our Lord for broken humanity is revealed. How quickly we forget.

A GUILTY HEART

When I think about the fact that Nneka slapped her husband, I ask, "What would Jesus do?" Then I remember that at the well in Samaria,

Jesus seemed to delight in talking to a notoriously sinful woman. She was openly living in sin after failing to find domestic tranquility with husband after husband after husband—five in all. She was not an orthodox Jew but a heretic, a Samaritan, following a mixed-up, pagan version of Scripture. But none of this was a barrier to His offer of a drink from the fountain of living water.

In fact, just the opposite. Jesus' door was wide open. *"But the hour cometh, and now is,"* He said to her, *"when the true worshippers shall worship the Father in spirit and in truth: for the Father seeketh such to worship him"* (John 4:23). This woman was being sought by the God of the universe. Her sin did not disqualify her to have a relationship with Him or to receive eternal life. And from these Scriptures, I can confidently say that Daniel's wife was not disqualified to receive anything in God's heart by her act of domestic violence.

I do not mean to downplay the seriousness of the offense. Quite the opposite. I am a realistic man. Through our marriage, my wife, Anni, and I have become one flesh before the Lord. But we are not of one mind. Our disagreements have had the potential to be as destructive as Daniel and Nneka's. By God's grace, we have been able to avoid that. However, I have had Christian married couples confess such failures to me during private sessions of tearful anguish. In the heat of disagreement, one partner or the other has lashed out physically, breaking the covenant of marriage in a moment of violent anger. In these sessions, one can sense how the fabric of love has been torn. Affections are wrenched with bitter disappointment and betrayal. The loose ends of the union are raw and bleeding. In such devastation, the enemy pours in his pernicious seed, and invisible scars form that can harden the heart beyond forgiveness.

A HARDENED HEART

In fact, that is what had happened to Daniel. In his mind, he said, *She has committed an abomination.* The more he thought about it, the more fiercely his anger burned. She was so wrong; and, by contrast, he felt so right. *Abomination* is a religious word applied to horrible sins—awful sins; things considered "beyond the pale." But we must stop to ask ourselves, *Does God see any sin beyond the pale?* May it never be! His sacrifice was sufficient to forgive every sin. Only one sin is unforgiveable, and that is blasphemy against the Holy Spirit. (See Matthew 12:31; Mark 3:29.) Nneka did not commit that unforgiveable sin when she slapped her husband in a show of disrespect. Whether her sin could be considered an abomination had nothing to do with the love of God. It was Daniel's pride that took the word *abomination* and created a barrier to forgiveness—a grudge that he would hold against her.

Daniel was a preacher of the gospel, a respected leader, and pastor of Power Chapel Evangelical Church in Onitsha. He should have known better. By denying forgiveness to Nneka, he committed a far greater sin than domestic violence. He would have done well to embrace the words of the apostle Paul, who urged us, *"And be ye kind one to another, tenderhearted, forgiving one another, even as God for Christ's sake hath forgiven you"* (Ephesians 4:32). Instead, Daniel hardened his heart.

A SIN UNTO DEATH

Please do not rush to the wrong conclusion. God did not kill Daniel for hardening his heart. Some of us might be inclined to think that, but God's Word is clear. He placed the sins of the whole world on His Son, Jesus, who was killed for us. We live under the New Testament, not the Old, and we have been purchased by His blood. We are no longer under the Law of Moses, with its endless curses and multitude of death penalties. Thank God! Hallelujah! He came that we might have life—abundant life; eternal life. (See John 10:10.)

So, what killed Daniel after he had hardened his heart? I will give you the answer in a name: Adam.

When you look at the scene of an accident, when you watch loved ones grow old and lose their ability to care for themselves, when you see a terrible birth defect, or when you look in a casket or gaze at a cemetery, you are seeing a result of the decision Adam made to eat from the Tree of Knowledge of Good and Evil. *"In the day that thou eatest thereof,"* God warned Adam, *"thou shalt surely die"* (Genesis 2:17). The death of all mankind came into this world through the fall of Adam. You and I were there, in Adam. Our DNA did not come from an ape or an amoeba. Adam, the first man, passed the sin nature to everyone born in every time and place thereafter.

Every person of every race, color, or creed is a sinner by birth. *"By one man sin entered into the world, and death by sin"* (Romans 5:12). But, praise God, we are told that through one Man, Christ Jesus, came redemption, atonement, the removal of our sins, the salvation of our souls, and the gift of eternal life. (See Romans 5:15.) We were born in sin, but we can be born again. This is the good news of the gospel that we preach in the face of the death of Daniel Ekechukwu. God did not punish him for his sin. God punished His only Son in Daniel's place.

Some will say, "Oh, but there is something the Bible calls *'a sin unto death'"* (1 John 5:16). From this Scripture, one might suggest that Daniel committed a sin unto death, for which God killed him. The full definition of a "sin unto death" is a discussion for another book, I'm sure. But even if you believe the worst case—that the unforgiveness in Daniel's heart toward his wife was, indeed, a sin unto death—it does not change my answer. God does not order someone's death as a penalty for committing sin. Death is the result of sin. *"The wages of sin is death"* (Romans 6:23), Paul wrote. God brings life. Sin and Satan bring death. (See John 10:10.) Upon these Scriptures I rest my case.

I will go on now to describe the car accident that killed Daniel, and the events that led up to it. We can only speculate about the effect of his state of mind on his alertness to danger as he drove. By his own admission, he was seething with anger toward his wife after a sleepless night of planning how to punish her. We are left to wonder, *With a clearer mind, could he have taken a wiser path and avoided the accident?* Perhaps so, but nothing good can come from that sort of question. It is simply impossible to know.

But of this we can be certain: None of us knows the day nor the hour of our appointment with death. Accidents happen. Sickness, old age, war, persecution, martyrdom, birth defects——all of these killers come to take us out of this fallen world, all thanks to sin. No one knows what lies ahead. That is why Paul, the "apostle to the Gentiles," wrote, *"Behold, now is the accepted time; behold, now is the day of salvation"* (2 Corinthians 6:2). I am an evangelist. I preach the day of salvation to millions, and to individuals, as well, one-on-one. I invite everyone to repent and bow at the door of salvation today. Receive God's gift of abundant, eternal life for all that is to come—*today*, not tomorrow. Now is the time. While you are still breathing.

A CLASSIC CONFLICT

This is the point in the story that inquiring minds want to know: the nature of the disagreement between Daniel and Nneka. What was it that sparked their heated argument? What prompted the slap and the resulting estrangement? In fact, it was a classic quarrel over the tensions that arise between the ofttimes conflicting obligation of a man to his family and to his career. In this particular case, the issue was Daniel's sense of calling to the work of the Lord. At the time of his incident, Daniel and Nneka had two sons, ages two and four, and she was pregnant with their third child.

Months earlier, he had scheduled a gospel crusade in a village some three hours away. The meetings would require him to preach from Monday through Wednesday. As he was preparing to leave, his youngest son had become ill. They had taken him to the local Catholic facility, St. Charles Borromeo Hospital, where the doctor had informed them that the boy needed minor surgery, and that a matching blood donor would be necessary before they could perform the procedure. Daniel had promptly allowed them to draw blood from his own veins. Then, after charging his staff at Power Chapel Church with looking after Nneka's need for transportation and helping with the children, he had left to conduct his meetings.

Nneka had felt deserted at a time when she especially needed her husband, and as she was shuttled back and forth between home and the hospital, her feelings of abandonment grew. She cried herself to sleep each night, until one evening when she received a promise—a moment of peace from the Lord. Something bright and beautiful came directly into her spirit. It was a vision of fruitful and fulfilling years with her husband. They were hand in hand, serving the Lord as one. It was not a vision perceptible to the natural eye, but it was so real that she could see their future together, glowing like a candle in the darkness. She embraced the promise and held it in the night, soon falling into a deep and restful sleep.

On Thursday evening, Daniel returned home. Nneka wanted to tell him about the promise, but he seemed distant. Her fears arose, and she was troubled. He asked her why she was not happy. Instead of telling him about the promise she had received, she explained her displeasure that he had left during a family crisis and had not come home even to check on her or the children. She told him that it felt like he was married to someone else, not her. He reacted by shouting, "What more do you expect from me? I paid for the doctors, I gave blood for the procedure, then I went to do the work of the Lord. What do you want? I have—"

It was at this point that Nneka slapped him. He was not finished defending his actions, but her slap ended his words. He walked away deeply offended. To his credit, he did not strike back, at least not physically. But in Nigeria, a woman is never allowed to slap her husband. In earlier generations, such an action could have resulted in her death. Daniel knew that no one would defend her if he made known what she had done. She had placed great power in his hands. She had no grounds on which to stand in the conflict. He held all the cards, and now he had to decide how best to play them out.

THE WAYS OF DEATH

Daniel went to his bedroom, removed Nneka's belongings, and announced that she would be sleeping in the guest room. Then he shut and locked the bedroom door. But he was unable to rest. His mind went round and round with the terrible offense he had suffered. The insult and disrespect could not be ignored.

Near midnight, he heard a tapping at the door. Nneka called through the latch, "My darling, please forgive me. I am so sorry. It was not me who slapped you. I don't know what came over me. It was the devil, I think."

He answered back, "Yes, it was the devil. And now that the devil has used you, he is through with you. But I am not through with you. Go away until I have decided what is to be done."

Before the night had passed, the answer came to him. He knew that Nneka loved him greatly. The distress that had led to her misbehavior had come from her being separated from him during the recent crusade. The perfect punishment, therefore, would be to send her away for an entire year. That would fit the crime and teach her to control her disrespectful outbursts in the future. With that resolve, he developed a plan to banish her to his father's house in the village of Amaimo, some seventy miles away.

In the morning, he dressed and left the house. As he passed by, Nneka approached him again with a cheery greeting, seeking to make amends. She had prepared breakfast for him and obviously wanted to apologize. He ignored her and walked to his car.

You will notice that this punishment is not what Scripture would recommend. There is nothing in the New Testament that would encourage Daniel to do anything but embrace his wife's apology and forgive her. But this man of God was acting according to his own plan. He was doing what he believed was right in his own eyes. When speaking about it years later, he would often quote Proverbs 16:25: "*There is a way that seemeth right unto a man, but the end thereof are the ways of death.*"

THE ACCIDENT

4

THE ACCIDENT

Before the subject of Nneka's yearlong banishment could be seriously considered, Daniel would have to mend some fences. His father, Mr. Lawrence Ekechukwu Ikugpe, was a village elder in Amaimo. In a land where the average lifespan is forty-seven years of age, he was a respected, old-school patriarch in his sixties with four wives. The extended family lived in a typical rural compound with individual houses for each wife and her children. But there was a longstanding difficulty between Daniel and his father, and it had recently taken a serious turn.

Daniel's father was a retired Baptist preacher, as well as a witch doctor. In fact, over the years, he had slipped backward from the pure faith into his tribal comfort zone, mixing Christianity with ancient traditions. Under the disappointment of not seeing prayers answered to his satisfaction, he had resorted to idols, fetishes, potions, and other superstitions—just to cover his spiritual bases, so to speak.

He did not recognize that two spiritual kingdoms existed, and that those kingdoms were at war with one another. Nor did he understand that God had defeated his enemy by raising Christ from the dead, and that all power in heaven and on earth had been given to His Son. (See Matthew 28:18.) As an elder and a shaman, he did not recognize that Christ had given His children *"power to tread on serpents and scorpions, and over all the power of the enemy"* (Luke 10:19).

Many superstitious people continued to come to him for cures and wisdom in dealing with day-to-day problems. He delivered his answers with a Bible in one hand and the trappings of witchcraft in the other. One might wonder if he had ever truly known the Lord at all. It is certain that Daniel considered him to be an unsaved man.

A SMOKING FLAX

Mr. Ikugpe's compromised religion resembled that of the Samaritans of Jesus' day (see John 4:7–22), that of the Jews who asked Aaron to give them a golden calf to worship at Mount Sinai (see Exodus 3:1–10), or that of the Galatian church of Paul's day, to whom he wrote, *"O foolish Galatians, who hath bewitched you, that ye should not obey the truth, before whose eyes Jesus Christ hath been evidently set forth, crucified among you?"* (Galatians 3:1). As an evangelist, I can really feel the apostle's frustration expressed in this passage—a frustration shared by many who have sown the seed of God's Word among tribal cultures. Those would include the twelve tribes of Israel, the barbarian Gauls known as Galatians, the many Celtic tribes of Europe, and the tribal roots that thrive in many parts of Africa today. In the United States, the Native American culture presents a constant challenge to the missionaries who labor among the various tribes.

The point I want to emphasize here is God's love for these people. Many missionaries and evangelists, including the apostle Paul and me, may have reached our wits' end, but God has never shared our frustration. He is long-suffering and infinitely patient, *"not willing that any should perish, but that all should come to repentance"* (2 Peter 3:9). He demonstrates amazing tenderness toward the "smoking flax" of tribal spirituality. (See Isaiah 42:3.) His gospel is as powerful to change a life in Africa as it is to change a life in the halls of enlightened idolatry at Oxford, Harvard, Princeton, or Union Theological Seminary—if not more so.

Often, in our mass crusades in Africa, there will be a night during which great bonfires burn. The people joyfully throw their idols, fetishes, and ritual books into the flames. They dance with freedom as they embrace the salvation that comes by grace through faith—plus nothing else!

In the story of Daniel Ekechukwu's resurrection, as it relates to the paganism of his extended family, I have seen the amazing love and patience of God demonstrated in the most tender ways. And that surprising tenderness is what I share with you in this book. Too often, we see God as ready to punish, ready to let the hammer of judgment fall on those in error. In truth, He stands at the door knocking, as He did with the Laodicean church in the book of Revelation. (See Revelation 3:20.) He is surprisingly near, ready to share His love feast with anyone who will open the door to Him.

Daniel's extended family, like many other families in Africa, had long struggled in a tug-of-war between the truth of the gospel and their old, familiar ways of tribal religion. Missionaries had come to Africa in the colonial era and had spread Christianity like the seed described in Jesus' parable of the sower. (See Matthew 13:3–9; Mark 4:3–9; Luke 8:5–8.) Some seeds fell on hard-packed earth, and birds ate it before it could grow. Other seeds fell on shallow ground and sprang up quickly, but then they died just quickly, because they had no depth of root. Some seeds fell among thorns and were choked. Other seeds fell in good soil and bore good fruit. It would seem that Daniel's father was an example of the seed sown among thorns. In time, the Word was choked by other cares, and he had backslidden into a mixture of paganism and Christianity.

THE TEENAGE PREACHER

At fourteen years of age, Daniel had heard the pure gospel at a crusade in nearby Owerri, a city of 200,000. There, he was drawn to the foot of the cross to receive Jesus. Soon after, he began to preach to his father about his need to repent, but it did not go over well. His father would wave his Bible at young Daniel and reply, "I was preaching from this Book before you were born. Don't tell me what is right or wrong."

Daniel's witness to his father was complicated by the normal tensions between teenagers and their parents. It was further complicated by the fact that, in this case, the teenager was right. It is a most difficult thing for a teenager to be right and the parent to be wrong about a matter of such importance. As a boy in Germany, I received a call to preach in Africa. My father was a minister of the gospel, sincere and true. Yet both of my parents discounted the value of my call. Through my teenage years, I struggled to hold firm to what God had spoken to me, without being disrespectful to my parents. It was a great challenge.

Daniel had a similar dilemma. By nineteen, he had become a full-time preacher. He moved from his rural home and started conducting gospel crusades in the surrounding nations of Africa, eventually establishing Power Chapel Evangelical Church in the city of Onitsha. In many ways, it appeared that he now stood head and shoulders above his father. He was the husband of one wife. His big, city church and crusades provided a better living than any career he could have undertaken in the small village of Amaimo. He could afford a Mercedes and the gasoline to operate it. He had disposable income. When he visited his village home, he was welcomed as a hero, and he could not resist the temptation to use his status to press the age-old conflict of his father's heresy. Still, Daniel loved and respected his father, and wished deeply that he would change. They shared many areas of common ground, including many tribal values, yet the old man remained staunch in his superstitions.

BLOOD FEUD

Tribal values run deeper in rural places, such as Amaimo, than in cities like Onitsha. For village dwellers, respect of one's elders stands as the pinnacle of pagan virtues. It extends, at the far extreme, to ancestor worship. Even though Daniel felt that he could differ with his father while still respecting him, some of his half brothers did not share this view. During a family visit some months earlier, they had overheard their father silencing Daniel with the same words he had used so many times: "I was preaching from this Book before you were born. Don't tell me what is right or wrong." To them, it sounded like Daniel had shown disrespect to the family patriarch. This was considered an abomination.

Further inflaming their anger, Daniel's mother had been Mr. Ikugpe's first wife, and she continued to hold a place of privilege over the other wives. In addition, she had given Daniel unfair advantages over the other children, not unlike Abraham's wife, Sarah, and her treatment of Ishmael. (See Genesis 21:1–11.) The resulting tension gave way to violence when Daniel's half brothers decided that Daniel needed to be taught a lesson.

When he visited the family compound, several of them attacked him, one so viciously that he was imprisoned by the police for attempted murder. As a result of the injuries he sustained in the attack, Daniel was taken to Umezuruike Hospital in Owerri. His recovery took days, and the wounds left scars on his face.

His extended family was still in turmoil over that violent episode on the Friday morning when Daniel decided to do something dramatic and heroic to calm the storm.

THE BRIBE

After shunning Nneka, Daniel decided to offer a peace offering to his father. Christmas was approaching, a season when he usually managed to exert a great deal of influence in the family with traditional gifts to celebrate the birth of Christ. With that in mind, he took a friend—a young man from his church—and drove his twenty-year-old Mercedes-Benz to pick up a prized goat. As is common in Nigeria, he loaded the goat into the backseat of the car and tethered it there.

This goat would be a special gift to his father, to be served as the main course at a family Christmas feast. He would also tell his father that he would put up the bail money so that his brother who was still in prison could attend, as well. He hoped this would be a powerful gesture of reconciliation, one that would rebuild the bridge of welcome to his extended family in Amaimo. He also hoped it would also pave the way for his banishment of Nneka.

It is easy to see that Daniel was contradicting himself—on the one hand seeking reconciliation with those who had persecuted him, while simultaneously seething in unforgiveness toward his wife. Hypocritical or not, his plan seemed to work. At the family compound in Amaimo, his father was so blessed by the gesture of the goat that he knelt down in the dirt and thanked God for his wonderful son. Daniel then gave both his father and his mother large gifts of money, after which he announced the sad news that Nneka had slapped him, then shared his plan to banish her to their compound for a year.

His mother made herself the champion of his cause by asserting without hesitation that he should do it. Plans were made for Daniel to bring Nneka to Amaimo for a visit on the following Sunday. When it came time to leave, he would inform her and the children that they would be staying with Grandpa and Grandma at the village. In a private session with Nneka, he would explain that this was to be her punishment for striking him, and that it would last a full year.

A DANGEROUS ROAD

With his primary mission accomplished, Daniel told his father that he would return with rice and vegetables to complete the Christmas feast, then he left to drive the seventy miles from Amaimo back to Onitsha, with his friend as passenger. As he came into his own neighborhood, he drove down a familiar steep gully.

It is important for those who have never driven in Africa to understand that even city streets and neighborhoods have very little asphalt paving. Except for the main arteries, nearly all the streets are dirt, and therefore subject to terrible erosion during the rainy seasons. Even a familiar lane can develop potholes that can nearly swallow a car. City street crews feel little obligation to fix these hazards, except in the areas of high traffic or perhaps in high-income neighborhoods, where those with political influence reside.

Daniel recalls passing, perhaps unwisely, a freight truck at the crest of the hill, which caused him to gain more speed than normal entering the gully. As he descended, he tried to brake but found that his brake pedal went to the floorboard, with no effect. He pumped it again and again, only to find his car out of control.

The car smashed head-on into a cement abutment that was designed to restrain cars from tumbling into the ravine below. Because Daniel wore no seatbelt, he was slammed against the steering wheel with great force. The impact threw his friend against the windshield on the opposite side of the car. He was injured but, miraculously, was not badly hurt. He looked across the car at Daniel and was aghast. The impact of the steering column against Daniel's chest had caused severe internal damage. He was bleeding from the nose and barely conscious. Soon, he began vomiting copious amounts of blood.

Daniel's memory is still unclear on the details of the accident, but he does recall hearing the sounds of the crowd that quickly gathered on the scene. Arms were pulling him from the smashed car and laying him on the ground. He heard conversations from bystanders describing his injuries as he continued to vomit blood from internal bleeding. He heard the voice of a woman volunteering her husband's car to be used as an ambulance to drive him to a local hospital.

A familiar face appeared above him, though, to this day, he is not sure who it was. Next, someone was running from the scene, crying loudly, and with great anguish, "Pastor Daniel! Pastor Daniel!"

NNEKA'S NIGHTMARE

5

NNEKA'S NIGHTMARE

Back in Onitsha, Nneka tried to find peace. She spent the day talking to God and reminding Him of a promise He had given her after Daniel had been viciously attacked by his family members. During his recovery in Umezuruike Hospital in Owerri, she had agonized over the terrible violence of his half brothers. In prayer, she had received a special assurance in her heart after reading these words from Isaiah: *"The sons also of them that afflicted thee shall come bending unto thee; and all they that despised thee shall bow themselves down at the soles of thy feet; and they shall call thee, The City of the LORD, The Zion of the Holy One of Israel"* (Isaiah 60:14).

Even though Nneka knew this Scripture had been written as a prophecy to Israel, she received the words as her own. They fit her painful situation and seemed to promise her that what Daniel's family had meant for evil, God would turn to an even greater good. (See Genesis 50:20.) In her heart, Nneka believed the Lord was speaking the word of Isaiah to her, promising her that she would not experience another violation. Her home would be called *"The City of the LORD."*

As she went about her housework that day, she declared her home to be the City of the Lord. She reminded God of His promise in Isaiah. She also asked Him what could be the meaning of the conflict between her and Daniel. To her further frustration, her husband had gone to make peace in his father's home—the very place where he had been so savagely beaten. In her relationship with God, she felt that she had the right to hold Him to the promise He had given her. But she was conflicted by the unforgiveness that remained in her marriage. In prayer, she asked, "What is this violation of my home? Why is it happening again? I hold You to Your promise, Lord. My home is the City of the Lord." But in that moment, the City of the Lord was coming under siege. A storm of evil was racing toward Nneka, one that would nearly capsize her faith.

She went to the kitchen and had begun preparing the evening meal when she heard through the open window the anguished cries of a young man running toward the house. Something about the sound of his voice grabbed her heart with the knowledge that something had happened to Daniel. She recognized the man as Kingsley Iruka, a neighbor who was also a friend from church. As he ran, he shouted, "It's Pastor Daniel! He's had a car accident. He's bleeding oh so badly!"

ANOTHER VIOLATION

As soon as Nneka heard these words from the street, her body gave out. She fell to the floor in a dead faint. This is a telling detail, I think. The stress that she was under must have been great. She felt the guilt of her action against her husband, for which she had twice tried to apologize. She also felt the added weight of his rejection. In addition to her prayers, her mind was wrestling with all kinds of negative self-talk, some true and some false. Her thoughts accused her one minute and blamed her husband in the next. Round and round the mental storm raged. Beyond all of this, she also was several months pregnant.

In times of distress, the flesh wants to become very active. We see this at work in the disciples as they crossed the stormy sea with Jesus asleep in the boat. In their desperation, they lost their belief that He cared for them. Their thoughts plunged them into a sea of doubt, and when they awakened the Master, He rebuked them for their lack of faith. (See Mark 4:35–41; Luke 8:22–25.) So it was for Nneka, left to her own thoughts for so long. Meanwhile, in her spirit, the love of God cried out against the nature of the quarrel. The heart of Christ bears no room for unforgiveness. Now, suddenly, the news that Daniel had suffered an accident drove her emotions beyond anything her body could endure, and she simply collapsed.

Concerned neighbors entered the home and found her unconscious on the floor. With cool water, they helped her recover. As soon as she was aware of her surroundings, her thoughts drove her to action again. She got to her feet, asked the neighbors to look after the children, and then followed Kingsley at a run back to the crash site.

At the sight of the wrecked Mercedes-Benz, her fears increased. She saw a lot of blood on the ground, but there was no sign of Daniel. Frantic, she questioned those at the scene, who told her that some bystanders had borrowed a car to take him to a hospital—St. Charles Borromeo Hospital, on the edge of the city. She knew the hospital well, for it was there that her son had received treatment for a recent illness. It was many miles away—too far to walk. And who would drive her? Even in a large city like Onitsha, automobiles are expensive. The cost of gasoline can be a large portion of a person's total income. It is never assumed that on a moment's notice, a car will be available for an emergency. Nearly beside herself with worry, Nneka returned to her house.

Kingsley tried to calm her fears and reassure her. He promised to find someone to drive her to the hospital.

THE FIRST HOSPITAL

As Kingsley searched for a car, Nneka made arrangements with a trusted neighbor to take care of her two sons in her absence. Soon, Kingsley returned with a driver who transported him and Nneka across the city to the hospital. They found Daniel in the intensive care unit, hooked up to an IV. The doctor explained that Daniel was having difficulty breathing and had lost a lot of blood. He also told her that he had been asking for her. She approached his bedside and knelt down.

"Pastor, Pastor, wake up," the doctor said. "Your wife is here."

Daniel opened his eyes, gazing through a haze of pain and medication. It took several long seconds before he could focus on her face. "Nneka," was all he managed to say.

"Do you want to leave me and the kids and just go to heaven?" she asked him. "I think you should not do that."

He asked, "Where am I?"

"You are at Borromeo Hospital."

On top of his painful injuries and his medicated state, he began to grow visibly upset. He motioned for Nneka to lean closer.

"Get me out of here," he whispered. "If you love me, you will take me from this place. They are doing nothing to help me. You've got to get me back to Owerri, to Umezuruike Hospital, where they know what to do. Dr. Misereke is the doctor there, and he is a friend of mine. He took excellent care of my injuries. He will know the right thing to do. Take me immediately."

Nneka fought the urge to weep. She wondered if Daniel's injuries had disturbed his thinking. Or perhaps the medication had muddled his mind. But he had not misspoken. He seemed to know exactly what he was saying. It seemed outrageous that he would want to travel the seventy miles again, this time with serious injuries. But Nneka took hold of her fears. Her husband had spoken; she had no desire to show the slightest disrespect toward him ever again.

When she told the doctor of the plan to relocate Daniel, he was shocked. He warned her that the ride could kill Daniel. In no way could he authorize a move across town, let alone to Owerri.

She told him she would secure an ambulance, so that a nurse could tend her husband as they drove.

Still not satisfied, he told her that Daniel was in very serious condition and could take a turn for the worse at any moment. He considered it insane to move him.

She returned to Daniel's side and told him what the doctor had said. "Do you still want me to take you there?" she asked.

He didn't hesitate, though he was laboring to breathe. "Yes," he said.

Her course was clear. It was now early evening. She made arrangements for an ambulance to make the transfer. When the doctor realized that she was serious, he brought her a legal form to sign, absolving St. Charles Borromeo Hospital from all liability. The form clearly spelled out that she was moving her husband against professional medical advice. She signed her name and was handed a plastic bag containing Daniel's personal effects. These included his wallet, a pocket watch, his wedding ring, and a cell phone.

KNOCKING ON HEAVEN'S DOOR

The route from St. Charles Borromeo to Umezuruike Hospital required navigating heavy city traffic. Ground transportation in Africa is always an adventure, but the risks of this trip were beyond calculation. The siren helped clear a path for the ambulance as it squeezed through bumper-to-bumper traffic and gridlocked roundabouts. Only a few intersections were monitored by traffic lights or policemen. The trip, which would have taken an hour without traffic, was going to take two hours or more.

They set out, Nneka seated in front between the driver and Kingsley. She wanted the nurse to remain in the back with her husband, in order to give him every possible advantage. As the trip progressed, however, her mind whirled with worries of the unknown. She had not received a detailed account of her husband's injuries, as the hospital, like most medical facilities in the region, was minimally equipped. The doctor had only his stethoscope to monitor the heart and the lungs; he did not have the benefit of EKGs, X-rays, MRIs or CAT scans. This is why Daniel's desire to have a particular doctor made sense to Nneka. In simple medicine, the skill of the doctor in charge can make all the difference.

Glancing back, she could see Daniel's chest heaving. He was struggling to force air in and out of his lungs. Had a broken rib punctured a lung, causing it to collapse? The internal bleeding was a very bad sign. So far, Daniel had not received any blood to replenish what he had lost. An intravenous saline drip had staved off dehydration, but every minute that passed without proper care seemed like an hour wasted. Nneka was troubled further by every jostling turn and chuckhole, which put more stress on Daniel's wounds. She couldn't escape the memory of her own hand signing the legal document at St. Charles Borromeo. All of the weight of this decision fell on her shoulders alone, making every mile seem like an eternity.

Before long, the nurse was tapping her on the shoulder. Daniel wanted her to come back and sit with him. She did not wait for the vehicle to stop but simply clambered over the seat and made her way to her husband's side.

Immediately, she could see that something had changed. Daniel looked worried. His complexion had taken on a pasty hue. He opened and closed his eyes, but they were cloudy, and seemed to want to roll back in his head and remain shut. He forced them open again, fighting to maintain consciousness, and motioned for her to come near.

"There is a box under my bed," he said. "It contains the important papers from the church." He spoke as if for the last time.

"Don't even think about that now," she pleaded.

"You will need to know how to handle the funds…how to deal with the church board. I have built a good house for you and the children."

"No, no, no." Nneka shook her head vigorously.

"You will need money to see to our boys and the child you are carrying. Nneka, some people are called to die young. I am one of them."

A reservoir of pent-up tears burst from her eyes, splashing across the stretcher. "No, Daniel! No, my husband. You are a man of God. You must speak faith and not doubt. You will live and not die. God has promised me a future with you."

Inside, Daniel sensed that he was dying. It was not unpleasant. He silently prayed that God would forgive his sins and receive him to heaven. But he could not hold on for Nneka's sake any longer. His eyes rolled back in his head, and he slipped into unconsciousness. The nurse checked his pulse and his breathing, but with the motion of the ambulance, she could not be certain that he was still with them. "Don't leave me!" cried Nneka. "You cannot leave. You will live and not die, in the name of Jesus! God has promised me! He has promised! He has promised!"

Finally, the truth set in: Daniel Ekechukwu was dead.

A PRAYER AND A PROMISE

In her mind, Nneka recalled that moment during Daniel's recent trip when she had received a promise, a moment of strange peace, from the Lord. She had seen a vision of fruitful and fulfilling years with her husband. When Daniel had returned from the trip, she had been eager to discuss it with him; but, before she had a chance, they had quarreled, and she had slapped him. Now the peace of God's promise seemed far away. Like a dream. Like a childish fairy tale. Like it had never happened.

In the ambulance, she reached down and touched Daniel's face. She was not prepared for what she felt. It was clammy and cold; there was absolutely no response to her touch. She felt beneath his nose and detected no breath of air. She suddenly felt very alone. A full, dark night had descended around them as they raced on toward Owerri, with siren blaring.

"Oh, Jesus," she whispered through cascading tears, "You promised. Remember Your promise to me. You promised."

The ambulance siren suddenly died as the vehicle lurched to a stop at the doors to Umezuruike Hospital. The driver and Kingsley leaped out, calling for emergency help. They burst through the main entrance and disappeared inside. Nneka remained with Daniel. The nurse exited the vehicle through the double doors at the rear and prepared to remove the stretcher, but it had no wheels; this was a job for two able-bodied people. Nneka waited. If only they could get him inside and get his circulation going again. Surely, there was some treatment that would make a difference. This is where they would find Dr. Misereke, the good doctor who would know what to do. One anxious minute turned into two, then three.

The ambulance driver emerged from the hospital, a look of disgust on his face. He signaled the nurse to close the rear doors of the vehicle, while Kingsley climbed back in the front passenger seat. "There is no doctor on duty," he said to Nneka. "They cannot accept emergency patients."

Nneka could hardly contain her frustration. "But can they call Dr. Misereke? He is Daniel's friend. He knows him."

"It's the doctor's day off," he replied helplessly. "Even doctors need time with their families."

"There is no other doctor?" she asked.

"There is no one," the ambulance nurse said, as she shut the rear doors. "We'll go to Federal Medical Hospital."

WILD GOOSE CHASE

The siren fired up again as the ambulance raced through the night across Owerri toward the city's largest hospital. Nneka struggled with terrible thoughts of self-loathing. Why hadn't she had someone call ahead to Umezuruike Hospital? If they had known the situation, they would not have wasted precious time; would not have taken the risk. Daniel himself might have agreed to stay at St. Charles Borromeo.

She wept as she massaged Daniel's cold hand and forearm. When she let go of his hand, his arm flopped lifelessly onto the floor beside the stretcher. "No, no!" she insisted, lifting the arm and laying it across his chest. Then, taking his other arm, she held both of them together with one hand, using the other to try to massage life back into them.

When the ambulance came to a stop outside Federal Medical Center, near downtown Owerri, Nneka glanced up at the building. It was large and impressive, and she thought that perhaps God had intervened in order to bring them to a better hospital. Even so, as she waited to hear from the staff, she experienced a sickening dread.

Soon the ambulance driver returned to the vehicle, looking dejected. The emergency room had shut down. As a government facility, it was against policy to accept accident patients at this late hour.

Nneka would not accept such an answer. She leaped out the rear doors and rushed into the hospital, screaming and crying, begging every staff member in sight to admit her husband. Finally, a doctor who had overheard the commotion emerged into the entryway. Fearing that her hysteria might upset other resting patients, he told her he would come out and make an examination in the ambulance. He brought a nurse with him. Using his stethoscope, he checked for Daniel's pulse—and then confirmed that he was dead. He gave the driver directions to the mortuary.

Nneka quickly shut herself inside the ambulance and instructed the driver to go to the home of her uncle, Okoronkwo Emmanuel, in Owerri. He knew other doctors in the city. She insisted that the Federal Hospital doctor was wrong and that Daniel still had a chance to live. The driver complied; after all, she was paying for his services.

Upon arriving at the Emmanuel residence, Nneka called her uncle out to the ambulance. She told him Daniel had been badly hurt in a car accident and needed to see his special doctor from Umezuruike Hospital. Mr. Emmanuel did not know anything about that doctor, but he offered to take them to his own doctor at the nearby St. Eunice Clinic. He insisted that he was a very good doctor—a Christian, a Catholic. Once again, the ambulance careened across the city toward its latest destination. Nneka's feelings of dread rose, nearly overwhelming her. She could hardly endure any more self-loathing for having taken Daniel from St. Charles Borromeo so that he could die on this wild goose chase. Still, her mind would simply not accept the fact that he was dead.

A DEATH CERTIFICATE

Arriving at the clinic, they found Mr. Emmanuel's doctor, Dr. Josse Anuebunwa, on duty. At last, Daniel's body was moved from the ambulance to an examination room. With Nneka, Kingsley, and Mr. Emmanuel standing by, Dr. Anuebunwa listened with his stethoscope for a heartbeat and found none. He felt for a pulse. Nothing stirred. He listened for lung function and heard nothing. Finally, he took his examining flashlight and forced Daniel's eyelids open. His gaze was fixed, his pupils dilated. In seventeen years of practice, Dr. Anuebunwa had seen enough death to recognize the signs.

"Your husband is dead, Nneka," he said. "I'm sorry. There is nothing more to do."

She sank to the floor, weeping in helpless anguish, feeling alone and betrayed—betrayed by God, by her husband, by her own actions, and by the evil circumstances of the accident. In that moment, however, she was left with something else. Something even deeper inside her refused to be extinguished by the relentless attack of death and destruction. It was the flicker of the promise she had received in the night, fanned to flame by the Scripture from Isaiah, telling her that her home would be called the City of the Lord. Could there be anything to it, now that Daniel was dead? Perhaps it provided something she could yet hold on to. But how? As Dr.

Anuebunwa began filling out a death certificate, she stared numbly at the paper.

Daniel was declared dead on Friday, November 30, 2001, at 11:30 p.m., at St. Eunice's Clinic in Owerri. The certificate detailed the examination results and listed the factors that had pointed to the conclusion of "demise." At the bottom of the certificate, the doctor wrote out his recommendation: "For removal to mortuary." Placing the full weight of his professional reputation on the line, he sealed the document with his signature.

NNEKA'S HOPE

6

NNEKA'S HOPE

According to tribal custom, as soon as Daniel was dead, his body no longer belonged to Nneka; it belonged to his father, Lawrence Ekechukwu Ikugpe. Before taking the body to the mortuary, she felt obligated to take it to Daniel's home village, to his father's house, which was only ten miles away. She felt helpless to do anything more. So, the ambulance became a hearse, transporting the body to Amaimo.

The village was nowhere near a main road. In fact, the final miles of the journey there were no more than a trail. The people who live in this region travel by foot. Some have oxen and carts, most have access to a bicycle, and a few have motorized scooters. Automobiles are the rare exception, and the road system reflects that fact. A hundred yards from the family compound itself, the ambulance was forced to stop at an open sewer, and the final distance had to be covered on foot. They arrived just after midnight. Nneka asked the nurse to open the rear doors of the ambulance. She remained there with the body as Kingsley went to find Daniel's father.

At the house, Kingsley called through the windows to awaken Mr. Ikugpe from sleep. In the Niger Delta region, houses have doorways but no doors; windows, but no glass. Curtains suffice, yet even those are considered a luxury. Temperatures in the tropical climate are comfortable, fluctuating between seventy and eighty degrees Fahrenheit, day and night. As Kingsley called out for Mr. Ikugpe, other family members were awakened. They came out of their houses and gathered in the common area near the main house.

At last, the patriarch of the clan hobbled into the yard, steadying himself with his cane. He immediately sensed that something was wrong. Kingsley told the shocking story of the accident and Daniel's subsequent death. The old man took it in, not sure he had heard correctly. Some of the others began to wail.

Mr. Ikugpe seemed in a daze as Kingsley led him back to the ambulance, lighting his way with a flashlight. At the vehicle, Nneka began to weep silently when she saw the old man. She knew well that Daniel's father had also been his spiritual adversary for many years. It was unthinkable to her that a representative of the true faith should be brought so low before a witch doctor. But what could she do?

She guided Daniel's father inside the ambulance to see his son's body. He reached out and felt the cold skin. Rigor mortis was already setting into the limbs. In the glow of the dome light inside the ambulance, his face appeared placid. It was then that the reality hit him, and he knew that this was the same son who had visited that very morning. Having accepted the death, he began to weep and cry aloud, while the rest of Daniel's extended family gathered around and joined in the chorus of agony.

Soon the entire neighborhood had awakened, and people came running from every direction to see what was causing the disturbance. As curiosity seekers pressed in all around the ambulance, Mr. Ikugpe suggested that he and Nneka take the body to the local mortuary for the night. It was only a mile from the family compound. And so, the ambulance was employed as a hearse yet again.

AT THE MORTUARY

The Ikeduru General Hospital Mortuary existed in a primitive village, much like the family compound at Amaimo. The mortician, Mr. Barlington Manu, lived next to the mortuary, a family business that had been passed down to him by his father. The mortuary primarily served the hospital in the neighboring village of Inyishi. Mr. Ikugpe knew Barlington Manu by reputation, having spent his entire life in the area.

Like most of the residential structures in the region, the mortuary building had no secure doors or windowpanes. Animals wild or domestic, including rodents, easily could have accessed the bodies inside, except that the chemical smell repelled them. Not even a fly could be observed landing inside the building. Over the generations, the Manu family had never had a corpse molested. Their livelihood depended on it.

They approached the house of Mr. Manu and called for him at the doorway. After several minutes, he came out of the house. Mr. Ikugpe explained that his son had just died and that he had brought him to be embalmed. Apprised of the situation, Mr. Manu started a gasoline-powered generator that illuminated the overhead lights in the mortuary for night work. Kingsley and the ambulance driver assisted him by carrying the stretcher with Daniel's body into the building.

There were dozens of other bodies in the mortuary, protected from decay by formaldehyde injections administered by Mr. Manu. There was no refrigeration, of course, and this was the time-tested method that preserved bodies in reasonable condition until the family could collect enough money to host a proper burial. One body in the building had been awaiting burial for five years.

They removed Daniel's body from the stretcher and placed it on a slab. Mr. Manu used a stethoscope to conduct his own examination of the corpse. When he had verified the validity of the death certificate, he informed Mr. Ikugpe and Nneka that he would proceed with the embalming process that night. He offered them his condolences, then added the body to his roster of cadavers. The record, which exists to this day, notes that Daniel was received on Friday, November 30, 2001. In fact, it was in the early hours of Saturday, December 1, that he arrived; but in this rural part of Nigeria, no one wears a watch, and so the night belongs to the previous day. In Mr. Manu's mind, it would not be Saturday until the sun came up. Daniel's father paid him one thousand naira to begin the embalming process.

EMBALMING THE DEAD

Nneka and her father-in-law traveled by ambulance back to the family compound in Amaimo. It was decided that she should stay there until funeral plans were finalized. The ambulance driver was paid, and the vehicle and nurse were released to return to their home base in Onitsha. Nneka was shown to a bedroom in Mr. Ikugpe's house where she could rest and try to get some sleep.

Meanwhile, at the mortuary, Mr. Manu summoned his assistant, who lived nearby, to help him prepare the body for storage. Next, he took a syringe and injected a formaldehyde mixture between the fingers and toes. The digits were beginning to curl, and the chemical would help relieve the rigor mortis. This procedure would also make the body easier to position for the main process of embalming. The next step involved using a hand pump to force a formaldehyde/water mixture into the circulatory system to replace the blood. To accomplish this, an incision would first be made on the inner thigh, so that a large catheter could be inserted into the femoral artery. This would provide access for the preserving chemical to enter the bloodstream. A large container of formaldehyde with a hand pump stood by for this purpose.

Another incision would then be made, and a second catheter inserted into a main artery on the opposite side of the body. A large basin was positioned there to receive the blood as it was expelled. The process would proceed slowly, and it would be repeated several times, until the chemical worked its way through the small capillaries and eventually permeated the soft tissue of the entire body. The chemical would eventually be absorbed by the skin, as well, preserving it from decay and naturally repelling any animal or insect that might be inclined to devour it.

DIVINE INTERRUPTION

As Mr. Manu made his first incision in the thigh, he received what felt to him like a strong electric shock. It knocked him backward with real force. He and his assistant looked at one another with concern. As practicing animists, they believed that all physical reality is permeated with spirits of various kinds—some evil, some benevolent, some neutral. In his work of embalming the dead, Mr. Manu held the spirit world in high regard, and he was not one to ignore signals that he was violating a territory held by an invisible host. He knew that Daniel's father, Mr. Ikugpe, was a local witch doctor, and he suspected that, through his father, Daniel had acquired powerful spirits that were interfering with the procedure. Mr. Manu thought that perhaps Mr. Ikugpe would be able to perform some ritual that could put an end to this spiritual mischief.

First, though, he decided to try making an incision on the other side of the body, thinking that perhaps the opposite thigh had not been attached to the same spirit. Again, the charge of electricity knocked him backward. This time, the signal left no doubt. His entire arm became numb from the shock, to the extent that he could not coordinate its movement for the rest of the night. Attempting any further work on the body would prove futile. He told his assistant that they would go to Mr. Ikugpe in the morning and ask him to perform some magic to pacify the invisible entities.

With that, he asked his assistant to help him carry the body into Room #2, where two other bodies lay on an elevated slab, awaiting embalming. They hoisted it onto the last available space on the slab, and then Mr.

Manu shut off the generator, watching the lights fade to black. He bid his assistant good night and returned to his house to resume sleep.

Back in his own bed, he found his wife sleeping soundly. But before he could close his eyes, Mr. Manu heard the sounds of a gospel choir singing and clapping in the night. It was a most unusual sound for that hour. He thought that perhaps the little church his wife attended, which was located several hundred yards beyond the mortuary, had decided to hold some kind of midnight vigil. He woke his wife and asked her if the church was meeting. She assured him that it was not.

He went out into the yard and, to his surprise, found that the singing seemed to be coming from the mortuary, not from the church beyond it. He shook his head with disbelief, then went to the door and peeked in. As he did, the singing stopped. Fear crept up the back of his spine to the base of his skull, causing him to shiver.

Determining to put it out of his mind, he returned to bed. When he closed his eyes, the singing resumed. As terrified as he felt, he simply could not ignore it. He had to identify the source of the singing. He got up again and retraced his steps across the yard to the mortuary. As he approached the door, the singing stopped. But he did not stop at the door this time. He entered the dark building, illuminated only faintly by starlight filtering in through the windows and doors, and headed for Room #2.

When he looked inside, the sight was unlike anything he had ever seen in all his years of practice. Daniel's face was glowing. Tiny points of light emanated from his skin and returned, as if performing some kind of light-particle dance. Mr. Manu looked to the window to see if the moon was casting a beam across the corpse's face, but the angle was such that the possibility was eliminated. He looked at the faces of the two other dead bodies on the slab. No such light came from them. Daniel alone was glowing. This manifestation was beyond Mr. Manu's ability to cope. He concluded that the powers at work in Daniel's body were too strong for him. He feared they would surely harm him if he attempted to embalm the body.

ANOTHER PROMISE

Meanwhile, in Amaimo, Nneka was sitting up in bed, reading her Bible by candlelight. On the page before her was Hebrews chapter 11, a passage famous for its list of Old Testament heroes of the faith. Suddenly, a phrase from the chapter nearly leaped off the page: *"Women received their dead raised to life again"* (Hebrews 11:35). The words quickened a powerful thought in her mind: *If Old Testament women received their dead raised to life again, why not me?* Daniel was dead. In the natural, there was no hope. But with God, all things were possible. (See Matthew 19:26; Mark 10:27; Luke 18:27.)

Her mind returned to the intimate moment with God in which she had received His peace and His promise. A new hope was born in her heart as she reread the Scripture from Hebrews. She had received a vision of a future with Daniel—the two of them serving the Lord together as one. That vision would be fulfilled only if this Scripture somehow became her own—if she became one of those women who received their dead raised to life again. She embraced her Bible and squeezed her eyes shut in the flickering candlelight.

"Oh, Father, Father," she prayed, "let me be one of those women."

NNEKA'S DREAM

7

NNEKA'S DREAM

On Saturday morning, Mr. Manu and his assistant arrived at Mr. Ikugpe's family compound. Nneka came out of the house with Daniel's father to meet them in the yard. The mortician placed the 1,000-naira note firmly into the old man's hand and then stepped back.

He said, "You must come remove the body from my mortuary at once. I cannot do my work."

Mr. Ikugpe replied, "Why can't you do the work?"

"Please, please," Mr. Manu said, "I tell you, there are strong forces around the body. Twice I tried to inject embalming fluid and was knocked back by an electrical shock. What have you done to make this happen?"

"What do you mean? I have done nothing," Mr. Ikugpe replied.

Nneka listened to this exchange with great interest.

Mr. Manu continued, "You have made a spell or some powerful witchcraft over the body. You have attracted bad spirits. They will not let me work."

"No, no. I have done nothing."

"Surely you have," Mr. Manu insisted. "You are a powerful elder who speaks with the ancestors. In the night, some of them were singing. What was the singing? I heard singing coming from the mortuary. Clapping and singing."

At this point, Nneka could not contain her excitement. She suspected that the body had attracted good spirits, not bad ones. "What kind of singing?" she asked. "Was it chanting and drumming?" In her mind, this type of noise would indicate an animist or voodoo ceremony.

"No, no. It was a like the hymns they sing at the church where my wife goes on Sunday. The church is just over the hedge from the mortuary. I thought they were singing in the night, but I woke my wife, and she said no. There was no church service at that hour."

Hearing this, Nneka was secretly thrilled. The singing of hymns meant to her that Mr. Manu had heard an angelic choir, and the idea gave her a surge of new hope.

"The song came from the mortuary," he continued. "And when I went to inspect it, the singing stopped. This happened not once but twice. And something more: I went inside to inspect the body, and Daniel's face was glowing with light. Small particles of light were circling in and out of the skin on his face. I have never seen anything like it in all my years of practice."

THE FLAME OF FAITH

Nneka knew the Scripture that describes God as light. The same verse goes on to declare that *"in him is no darkness at all"* (1 John 1:5). The Bible makes it clear that the kingdom of light rules above the kingdom of darkness. In her mind, that Daniel's face had been glowing with light seemed to indicate that God was at work, not the prince of darkness. A spark of hope began to generate a flame of faith inside her.

As it turned out, Mr. Ikugpe had his own interpretation of the light on Daniel's face. "This light, I can explain," he said, waving his ceremonial cane. "I know what you are seeing. My son was a man of God—a preacher of the gospel. That is why there is light on him. I did not do anything."

"That is right," Nneka said. "I believe it is a sign that God will raise him from the dead," she added.

Mr. Ikugpe and Mr. Manu were too stunned to reply.

"Last night," she continued, "I received a Scripture from the book of Hebrews. It says, '*Women received their dead raised to life again.*' I believe this is what God will do for me."

"Grief is making you mad," her father-in-law said. He spoke as if it was an obvious matter of fact. "That is what is going on with you. You are not in good balance. Daniel is dead. He will not rise again!" He spoke with the authoritative voice patriarchs often use to assert leadership over their extended family, including their wives—a tone that usually signals the end of a matter.

But Nneka's faith was beginning to make her bold. She replied quietly, "If God has promised me something, Daddy, do you want to be the one who stands in His way?"

Mr. Ikugpe remained silent. He considered his answer carefully. Though he was an animist, he thought of himself as one of God's helpers, not His enemy. "The doctor said he was dead," he replied at last. "Mr. Manu said he was dead. If they are wrong, then someone has placed Daniel under a voodoo curse, like the curse of a zombie. I have a ritual for that, and I can find out if it is true. I will take my Bible and hit him on the head seven times. If he is a zombie, he will rise. If he is dead, then there is nothing anyone can do."

"This is good," Mr. Manu said, "but you must please hire another ambulance and remove the body today. It must be gone before it begins to decay. Come now and do this. I am afraid of these things that are going on. I want nothing more to do with it."

"We will come today, and I will bring my Bible," Mr. Ikugpe promised him.

THE ZOMBIE RITUAL

The long trek to the mortuary proceeded slowly. Mr. Ikugpe walked with his colorful cane, a ceremonial symbol that had been given to him by his father, who had received it from his own father. All of them had been animist priests. Nneka walked beside him. A young half brother of Daniel's walked on his other side, holding an umbrella over the patriarch's head, to shade him from the sun. Mr. Ikugpe had asked Nneka to bring Daniel's cell phone.

"Use the phone to hire an ambulance from Owerri," he ordered her. "I will pay for it. We will have him removed to St. Eunice's Clinic Mortuary, where he was pronounced dead. And we will tell them nothing of this that has happened with Mr. Manu. Do you understand?"

"Yes, Daddy," Nneka said.

As they walked, she began shopping by cell phone for an ambulance in Owerri. While she was unable to find one available on Saturday, she managed to secure one for Sunday. The driver told her that he was familiar with the location of the Ikeduru General Hospital Mortuary, and he agreed to meet them there in the morning.

They entered the mortuary with Mr. Manu and his assistant. He showed them to Room #2 and to the slab Daniel shared with two other corpses. Mr. Ikugpe tested Daniel's limbs for rigor mortis. His son's body was quite stiff. He then mumbled an incantation that he alone understood and struck Daniel on the head with his Bible. After some more mumbling, he struck him again. He repeated the process seven times. At the end, he turned to Nneka and said, "He is dead. That is the end of the matter."

"Yes, Daddy," she said, "it is the end of what you can do. But it is not the end of what God can do." Again, Nneka's faith expressed itself with boldness.

"I am a man of God," her father-in-law protested. "Daniel is a man of God. I hit him with the Bible seven times. He did not rise up. What is God going to do for you?"

"I don't know," she said. "But in the Bible, women received their dead raised to life again by the power of God. I am a woman. That is what I believe will happen."

Mr. Ikugpe felt sure that Nneka had slipped over the edge of sanity. He shook his head sadly and looked at Mr. Manu. "We will remove the body in the morning to another mortuary. Will you please hold Daniel for one more night?"

Mr. Manu did not appear comfortable with this idea, but he agreed, reluctantly. "But he is not embalmed, and flies will be attracted to the corpse," he said. "I cannot allow that. I will pack his nostrils with cotton to keep the insects from crawling inside and laying eggs. This is a great risk for me, professionally, to have him here without being embalmed."

"I will pay you for whatever you have to do to keep him here until we can come in the morning," Mr. Ikugpe assured him.

"Very well."

THE DIVINE APPOINTMENT

Nneka announced that she would fast and pray at the family compound for the rest of the day. Coincidentally, at the same time, I was fasting and praying in my hotel room in Lagos, seeking guidance for the decision of whether to relocate the headquarters of Christ for All Nations. At this point, neither of us dreamed that our paths were going to cross in about twenty-six hours.

When they arrived at the compound, Mr. Ikugpe insisted that Nneka's two sons be brought from Onitsha. He wanted Nneka to accompany him in a taxi to pick up her sons at the neighbor's and escort them to his compound. In his mind, Nneka was acting irresponsibly, chasing after the resurrection of her husband when she needed to tend to her motherly duties. He hoped that bringing the children to the compound and putting them under her care would force her to act more responsibly. Before leaving to get the boys, Nneka called the family together and asked them to tell the boys that their daddy was away in the village. This would not be a lie, she explained. She didn't want them traumatized in the meantime.

By late afternoon, Nneka had been reunited with her two boys. Her plan seemed to work. They were told that their father was away in the village. As children do, they played and carried on normally all afternoon, until they grew tired and ready for sleep.

As night fell on Saturday, Nneka put her sons to bed in a separate bedroom. She, too, was exhausted. The trauma of the previous day, plus the lack of sleep the night before, was finally catching up with her. Unable to hold her eyes open any longer, she entered her bedroom and collapsed on the bed. At some point in the night, she had a vivid dream, in which Daniel's face appeared, and he spoke to her: *"Why have you left me in the mortuary? I am not dead. I want you to remove my body and take it to the Reinhard Bonnke meeting at Grace Cathedral tomorrow."*

Immediately, she felt fully awake. The force of the dream was such that she could not stop herself from weeping aloud. Her tears were not just tears of sorrow but tears of fear mixed with hope. The pieces were beginning to fit together in a fantastic puzzle. The promise from God of a future with Daniel, the Scripture saying that women received their dead raised to life again, the singing in the mortuary, the light on Daniel's face, and now this dream of Daniel speaking to her—the signs seemed to be telling her that God was at work to raise Daniel, and she did not want to miss her part in the event.

In all of her recent trauma, she had found no time to consider the fact that I was returning to Onitsha to speak at the dedication of Grace Cathedral. She had not forgotten, but it had not seemed relevant to the difficulties she faced. Daniel's words in the dream sparked her memory, raising the faith in her heart to another level. Both she and Daniel had attended the Christ for All Nations crusade in Onitsha the previous spring, and she recalled that many people had accepted Jesus as Savior, and that many were miraculously healed, when I preached. No one she knew in Onitsha had ever seen anything like it.

The congregation of the church Daniel pastored, Power Chapel, had gained many new members in the wake of the crusade. Nneka also remembered what she had been taught at the Fire Conference and how powerfully she had felt the Holy Spirit in that gathering of believers. In her words, she became convinced that night that "Reinhard Bonnke carried an anointing that would raise Daniel from the dead." This was an idea that would not have occurred to her if her husband had not appeared and made his request to her in a dream.

Nneka was filled with a determination to do as he had asked. She believed that if she could get his body to Grace Cathedral the next day, God would use my prayer to raise him from the dead. To her, it was like the determination of the woman in Scripture who had struggled through the crowd to reach Jesus and touch the hem of His garment. When the woman attained her goal, she received healing from an incurable disease. Jesus turned to her and told her that her faith had accomplished this miracle. (See Matthew 9:20–22; Mark 5:25–34; Luke 8:43–48.)

Likewise, Nneka fixed her mind on getting me to pray for Daniel. She believed that an atmosphere of faith—or, as she called it, "an anointing"—would be present at the meeting and would bring her husband back to life. She had already arranged for an ambulance to take his body to another mortuary, so she would simply redirect it to Onitsha. If only Daddy, Mr. Ikugpe, would allow it.

THE SLEEP OF DEATH

Nneka's weeping had awakened Mr. Ikugpe. Standing at the door to her bedroom, he asked if he could enter. She gave him permission. When he came into the room, he asked why she was crying. She told him of the dream and begged him to let her take Daniel to my meeting in Onitsha.

He was not happy to hear this. "Daughter, I don't want to see you like this. Your grief has carried you away. The body must be embalmed and buried. I cannot let you disgrace Daniel like this."

"Oh, Daddy, please, please. I am not doing this. God is working, and I am obeying what He wants us to do. There is hope."

"I will not hear another word. My son's body will not be dragged around, humiliating our family. In the morning, we will get the body and take it to the mortuary in Owerri. That is my final word on the subject."

Nneka did not sleep another wink. Her tears flowed all night. Every few minutes, she would go to the window and peek at the eastern sky, willing the sun to rise so that she could return to the mortuary and put Daniel in the ambulance. She secretly pledged that if Daniel's father would not agree to direct the ambulance driver to take his body to the church in Onitsha, she would pay the ambulance attendants herself to change course and drive her there with the body.

This plan gained further strength in her mind because of something Daniel had said to her in the dream—something strange that she still did not understand. He had said that he was not dead. Every physical sign said he was dead, but in her dream, he had stated clearly that he was not. He had also expressed displeasure with being left in the mortuary. The electrical shocks, the singing, and the light emanating from his face in the night had kept Mr. Manu from embalming the body. These signs seemed to support the truth of this idea. Something in the invisible realm was testifying that, indeed, Daniel was not dead. Yet in the physical realm, he seemed very dead. He was not breathing; he had no pulse; his pupils were fixed and dilated; his limbs had stiffened.

Many times, Nneka had read the biblical account of the death of Jairus's daughter. (See, for example, Luke 8:41–42, 49–56.) When all the mourners were weeping over the little girl's body, Jesus had entered the house and said, "*Weep not; she is not dead, but sleepeth*" (Luke 8:52). The mourners in the house thought He was crazy. They laughed Him to scorn. Then, the Lord took the dead girl by the hand and raised her to life again. Jesus had told the truth about her being asleep. It was the sleep of death. In the physical, she was dead; but to God, her condition was temporary, like sleep. In truth, death is temporary for everyone. One day, all will be awakened from the grave. They will live forever, with eternal reward or eternal punishment.

In another instance, Jesus told His disciples that His friend Lazarus of Bethany was asleep—and that, by "asleep," He meant "dead." (See John 11:11–14.) When they arrived at Lazarus's house, they were told that he had been dead in the tomb for four days. (See John 11:17, 39.) Jesus said, *"I am the resurrection, and the life: he that believeth in me, though he were dead, yet shall he live: and whosoever liveth and believeth in me shall never die"* (John 11:25), and then He called forth Lazarus from the grave. (See John 11: 43–44.)

In a similar way, Daniel exhibited all the natural signs of being dead; but perhaps, as Jesus had said, he was merely asleep—in which case, Nneka could imagine receiving her dead husband raised to life again, just like in the Bible!

There was yet another detail of Nneka's dream that strengthened her faith. If Daniel was truly dead, then it meant that his father had tribal and legal authority over the body. However, if Daniel was merely asleep, Nneka, as his wife, had ultimate authority. Spiritually, his body belonged to her, not to his father, the preacher/witch doctor.

NNEKA'S FAITH

8

NNEKA'S FAITH

From the moment Mr. Ikugpe got out of bed on Sunday morning, he could not find a moment's peace. Nneka was ready and waiting for him. Through the night, she had become convinced that God was revealing His direction for her. She began to make her case, and she would not quit.

She told him that he should pay attention to all the signs that God was going to raise Daniel from the dead at Grace Cathedral: First, God had promised her. Next, He had prevented Daniel's body from being embalmed. Then, Mr. Manu had heard an angelic choir singing in the mortuary and witnessed Daniel's face glowing with light. Finally, Daniel had appeared to her in a dream, telling her that he was not dead and that he wanted her to take him to Grace Cathedral for the Reinhard Bonnke meeting. She insisted that her dream had been real, and that it was no coincidence I was preaching in Onitsha that day. It was part of God's plan, a divine appointment. They simply had to take Daniel there.

Mr. Ikugpe became more and more convinced that Nneka was mad with grief and could not be trusted. In his mind, the only thing that could bring her to her senses would be to see Daniel placed in a casket and buried in the ground. Secretly, in the early morning hours, he had sent one of Daniel's half brothers to the mortuary with enough money to buy a casket. He decided he would have him buried immediately after his embalming at the St. Eunice's Clinic Mortuary in Owerri. He hoped that this would shock Nneka back to reality. He told her to bring a plain white suit of Daniel's for burial. He further insisted that she bring along her older son to the mortuary. His hope was that she would hold her tongue to keep from upsetting him.

His plan did not work.

The long walk to the mortuary provided more opportunity for Nneka to press her position, which she did, in spite of the fact that her son heard everything. When Mr. Ikugpe stood his ground, she began to weep and plead all the more fervently. He had never faced such resistance to his leadership, and he began to fear that nothing would bring her to her senses. Her unflagging insistence began to shake his sense of being in charge of the situation.

When they arrived at the mortuary, he finally agreed to let her take the body to Grace Cathedral before it was embalmed, thinking that it would put her ideas of resurrection to rest. Given the way she was acting, he feared that if he didn't take that step, he would never hear the end of it as long as he lived—for if Daniel was dead, he was doomed to house Nneka under his roof for the rest of her days.

ROAR OF A LIONESS

The ambulance was waiting for them at the mortuary. Nneka informed Mr. Manu that they would be taking Daniel to Grace Cathedral for prayer, and that if he didn't rise from the dead, they would come back to Owerri to have the body embalmed and buried.

Mr. Manu seemed disturbed by this plan. He took Mr. Ikugpe aside and explained that if the authorities caught them transporting a dead body that had gone so long without being embalmed, they would arrest them on any number of charges—abuse of a dead body, or even suspicion of murder. Sometimes, the police would arrest people on mere suspicion and hold them as a bribe, until bail was received for their release. Mr. Manu did not want to give the authorities such an opportunity. In order to avoid accusations of being body snatchers, he suggested they transport Daniel in his grave clothes inside the coffin. Mr. Ikugpe assured him that they would bury him in the coffin they had purchased; therefore, transporting him inside it would be no problem. Nneka understood his position and agreed to it.

Mr. Ikugpe made it clear to Nneka that the entire situation offended him deeply, not to mention violated his tribal obligations. He also informed her that the responsibility for the situation was on her shoulders alone. Therefore, he made her pledge that if Daniel did not rise from the dead at Grace Cathedral, she would cover the burial costs in full.

Nneka readily agreed. In her heart, she never expected to pay a single naira.

Daniel Ekechukwu, laid out in his coffin.

By this time, the corpse was very stiff and difficult to dress. His arms and midsection were so stiff, they could not manage to get the shirt in place. Mr. Manu slit the back of the shirt with scissors and unbuttoned the front in two pieces. He put one half over one arm, the other half over the other arm, and buttoned it up in front. He then tucked the ragged backside under the body. From the front, everything looked rather neat and tidy.

Mr. Manu asked if he could accompany them to Grace Cathedral, now that they had committed to go. He had witnessed the strange phenomena around Daniel's body. He had also been present for Mr. Ikugpe's voodoo Bible ritual, which had failed. As an animist, he was curious to see what would happen next. If Nneka had received some kind of plan that would result in Daniel's resurrection, he did not want to miss it. He offered to follow the ambulance in his car. Mr. Ikugpe agreed, then suggested he transport Nneka and her son, as well.

Secretly, Nneka vowed that she would have none of this idea. She did not trust either man to follow through with her plan. But she did not argue the point, realizing that they would not willingly accept her refusal. Once they had loaded Daniel's coffin in the ambulance, she took her son by the arm and ran to the passenger side of the ambulance. Daniel's half brother and the driver blocked her way, took her by the arms, and tried to escort her to Mr. Manu's vehicle, but she turned on them and fought with the ferocity of a lioness.

"I will *not* be separated from my husband!" she screamed. "Do you understand?"

No one doubted her resolve; they decided not to press it further. She climbed into the ambulance with her son, while Mr. Manu and Mr. Ikugpe got into the car that would trail behind. Thus, the caravan began its seventy-mile journey to Grace Cathedral in Onitsha.

JOURNEY IN REVERSE

As the miles passed and they drew nearer to Onitsha, Nneka could not help but remember the heart-wrenching journey she had made just forty-eight hours ago. She had signed her husband out of St. Charles Borromeo Hospital because he had asked her to take him to Umezuruike

Hospital in Owerri to receive better care. The hospital had made her sign a release form, absolving the staff of all responsibility. She recalled the terrible anxiety that had plagued her on that trip—a journey that had resulted in her husband's death.

Now she returned along the same road in the opposite direction. Only this time, she was moving in response to another request her husband had given to her, in a dream. This time, she did not feel anxiety but an assurance that she was doing what God would have her do. She would not be knocked off course by circumstances. This journey would result in life, not death.

The caravan arrived at Grace Cathedral around one in the afternoon. Nneka could hear my familiar voice being projected through the loudspeakers. I was in the middle of my sermon about the river of God, exhorting the crowd to swim in the full stream of the Holy Spirit, letting it sweep them to new destinies in Christ. In her mind, Nneka saw herself driving the ambulance up to the main entrance, bringing the coffin to the front, and calling on me to lay hands on her husband and to raise him up. Little did she know that a number of government security officers would have a very different idea.

The ambulance was halted by armed guards before it could enter the parking zone. Officers came to each window. The man at the driver's window asked about the nature of the visit. Nneka began to spill out her story, feeling desperate now that she was so close—within earshot of my voice yet unable to continue. The officers jerked the doors open on both sides of the car and ordered her and the driver out. They had much less respect for her story than either Mr. Ikugpe or Mr. Manu. Behind her, she could see the other two men with officers at both windows of the car. Nothing was going according to her plan.

The first officer used his radio to call for backup. Soon, a large group of soldiers came running from the upper parking area. In the lead was the Muslim head of security, wearing dark sunglasses. They came with rifles leveled at Nneka and the driver, taking strategic positions around both vehicles in case of trouble. She continued to tell her story, not understanding the extra security measures that were in place because of my visit. She could not see how outrageous her story sounded to an objective observer under the circumstances. To the security forces, she seemed it sounded like a desperate plot to kill me with a bomb.

"My husband is a man of God!" she screamed. "He has had an accident, and Bonnke will pray, and he will rise up."

The security chief looked at his lieutenant and said, "Shut her up."

FLOGGING THE LIONESS

The officers began to shove Nneka roughly and told her to shut up, but she would not stop. She repeated her claim, again and again. Then they began to beat her with clubs, careful not to disfigure her face. They beat her arms, legs, and torso, front and back, calling her names and laughing at her stupidity. Soon she was knocked to the ground, where they kicked her mercilessly. Her son began screaming in fear. The commotion grew so loud that I could hear it inside the building as I preached on the platform. But, as I said, I am used to disturbances when preaching in Africa. I remained focused on my sermon.

At the same time, a group of people gathered around Nneka, most of them having been barred from the building because it had reached maximum capacity. Also among them were some of the church elders who were serving as parking attendants. They saw the security chief drag the coffin from the back of the ambulance and remove the lid. One of the elders, hearing what Nneka had said, ran back into the church to get help.

Meanwhile, the security chief ordered some of his men to take the body from the coffin and inspect it, top to bottom. Daniel's body was lifted out and placed inside the overturned coffin lid. The shirt, having been cut and tucked under the body, fell open. They removed it and inspected the body thoroughly. As they were doing this, others patted down the coffin itself, turning it over to see if it contained any kind of explosive material. They ripped apart the satin lining to inspect the wood for hidden compartments.

The security chief took hold of both of the cotton plugs protruding from Daniel's nostrils and jerked them free. With his flashlight, he looked up inside the nose to see if it had been packed with explosives. A portable explosive detection kit was used to test anything that seemed suspicious. Finally, when the inspection was over, the security chief seemed puzzled. There were no explosives—not in the cars nor in the coffin nor on the body. Nothing made sense to him now except Nneka's explanation, so he went to her and asked her to repeat her story.

She was in pain from the beating but had managed to get to her feet again. "My husband is a man of God," she repeated. "He had an accident and died, but God has told me that if I can get him to Bonnke, he will rise from the dead."

The security officers began to mock her again and rained down a new round of blows with their clubs. But this time, she would not be defeated. She continued to scream at the security chief, "I am telling the truth! Do not stand in God's way. Bring my husband into the church!"

Mr. Manu and Mr. Ikugpe had remained near Mr. Manu's car. They were frisked, while the car was searched. The two men made no attempt to come to Nneka's aid. They explained to the officers that Nneka was a grief-stricken widow, and that they were merely humoring her. She was the only one insisting that the corpse would rise from the dead in the church. In their view, she had brought this humiliation on herself, and they had tried to stop her. Both of them believed that Nneka had reached the end of her insane journey and would now be sent home to bury Daniel.

BLESSED INTERVENTION

But something happened that turned the entire situation in a new direction. The elder who had run to the church now returned with Pastor Paul's son. This man was in charge of security for the church and was well-known to the security chief. When he learned the identity of the corpse— the pastor of Power Chapel Evangelical Church, with whose reputation he was familiar—he asked to speak with Nneka and was led to where she stood. Speaking in kind tones, he asked her to repeat her story. She did. When Nneka pleaded with him to let me lay my hands on him and pray for him to rise from the dead, he told her that would be impossible.

Yet, as he listened to her, he sensed her sincerity. And he did not want to stand in the way of God if He had chosen to do something miraculous. He asked that the coffin be placed back in the ambulance and kept out of sight. He felt that if it remained in the open, it would be a disturbing image for the children who were being tended in the nursery area. He then suggested that the best course of action would be to take Daniel's body to the walkout basement entrance at the rear of the building. They could bring it into a vacant room without disturbing the dedication service in the main auditorium.

This seemed to be a wise and brotherly approach, under the circumstances—a solution that would relieve Nneka of her burden and also spare the Grace Cathedral crowd the distraction of having a dead body placed in the spotlight. I honestly don't know what I would have done if Nneka had been allowed to interrupt my sermon and bring Daniel to the front. The sensational nature of such a moment surely would have taken the entire event captive. My belief is that I would have heard from the Holy Spirit, and I would have obeyed His instruction, whatever it was. That is how I want to operate in all situations. But we will never know.

At the time, I was preaching under the anointing of the Holy Spirit, and I was aware of many powerful moments of ministry among the 10,000-plus people who had gathered there. Each of those precious souls had equal importance with Nneka's situation. As an evangelist, I felt an obligation to them. That is why I had not allowed the loud disturbance in the parking lot to interrupt my sermon.

THE BREATH OF LIFE

According to the suggestion of Pastor Paul's son, Daniel's body was carried, by a group of elders and security officers, into the basement entrance at the back of the cathedral. Once inside, they pushed two narrow tables together and laid him on his back on top of them. The shirt that Daniel had been wearing in the casket was in pieces and had become difficult to keep in place, so it was simply set aside. Two members of the church ministry staff began to lead the others in prayer for Daniel.

At this point, someone with a video camera had begun filming. In the footage, Nneka can be seen sitting quietly in the background. She had endured so much by this point and no doubt felt that her mission was accomplished. She had obeyed the instructions she'd received from her husband in the dream. She could hear my voice preaching in the auditorium above. The anointing to raise the dead was present in the building. She had touched the hem of the garment of the Lord, so to speak. The only thing she had not accomplished was getting me to lay hands on Daniel. Nor had she managed to get word to me to pray for this dead preacher in the basement, whose wife believed he would rise from the dead. In the video, she is seen sitting with her son, Mr. Ikugpe, and Mr. Manu, while members of the church ministry staff pray over Daniel's body.

At some point near the end of my sermon, something began to happen to Daniel. The video cameras captured it. His diaphragm began to move slightly, drawing air into his lungs and expelling it. In and out; in and out. At the sight, pandemonium began to break loose in the basement, and it spilled into the surrounding areas. Soon, people were rushing upstairs to let others know what was happening in the basement.

"He's breathing! He's breathing!" they shouted.

The Muslim security chief forced his way into the basement and through the crowd, making his way to the table where Daniel lay. He removed his sunglasses and bent down to look closely at Daniel's bare torso. He saw the motion of his diaphragm. He placed his finger beneath Daniel's nose and felt the movement of air through the passages that had recently been clogged by cotton. Eyes wide with wonder, he stepped away and put his sunglasses back in place. Nodding once to Nneka, he made his way out of the room to the security convoy that was waiting to escort me to the chartered airplane at the Onitsha airport.

I think it is divine irony that this happened at the approximate moment Daniel had planned to leave Nneka at his father's house to begin her yearlong banishment. Instead of granting him success in punishing his wife, God used that amazing woman to bring him to Grace Cathedral and back to life again. Hallelujah!

Since this miracle has received worldwide publicity, many have asked me to travel the world to pray for dead bodies. My response is that I am an evangelist. My calling is to preach the gospel to the living dead and let the Holy Spirit give new life to those who respond. Incidentally, Pastor Paul told me later that, had he known what God had in mind to do for Nneka and Daniel on that day, he would have thrown open the main doors and invited the coffin into the sanctuary for all the world to see! That is 20/20 hindsight for all of us. But God, in His wisdom, had other plans.

It all bears the fingerprints of the Almighty, I think. His Son was born in a lowly livestock stable, heralded by angels who sang to night-shift shepherds—not to kings or religious leaders. Why would He not choose to resurrect Daniel Ekechukwu through the back door of Grace Cathedral in a way that would leave us "big shots" out of the loop? The apostle Paul said, *"But God hath chosen the foolish things of the world to confound the wise; and God hath chosen the weak things of the world to confound the things which are mighty"* (1 Corinthians 1:27). In Luke's gospel, we find Jesus suddenly looking up to the heavens and shouting with great joy, *"I thank thee, O Father, Lord of heaven and earth, that thou hast hid these things from the wise and prudent, and hast revealed them unto babes"* (Luke 10:21).

Yes, I believe this unlikely path to resurrection bears His fingerprints.

RESURRECTION

9

RESURRECTION

What does a resurrection look like? Do you have a particular image? A formula? A prescribed notion of how God should do it?

Perhaps there are no two resurrections alike. Elijah lay on the dead son of the widow of Zarephath three times, asking God to revive him. He was revived on the third prayer. (See 1 Kings 17:21–22.) A dead body was placed in the tomb of Elisha the prophet and revived as soon as it made contact with his bones. (See 2 Kings 13:21.) Jesus raised Jairus's daughter, taking her by the hand. (See Matthew 9:25; Mark 5:41; Luke 8:54.) He raised Lazarus by calling him from the grave. (See John 11:43.) An angel descended from heaven and rolled away the stone from Jesus' tomb, and those who saw it fell unconscious. (See Matthew 28:2–4.) On that same night, Old Testament saints were seen emerging from their graves in Jerusalem and speaking to people in the streets. (See Matthew 27:52–53.) Peter knelt at the bed of Tabitha (also called Dorcas), who had died, and called her to life again. (See Acts 9:40.) The apostle Paul taught that the dead in Christ will one day rise from their graves to meet the Lord in the air. (See 1 Thessalonians 4:15–17.) Finally, while the apostle Paul preached an all-night sermon, a boy named Eutychus fell from a window three stories to his death. Paul lay on top of him, embraced him, then got up and told everyone not to worry; the boy's life was still in him. The next morning, after Paul had eaten breakfast and continued on his journey, Eutychus was brought back into the meeting place and presented alive and well. It apparently took some time for that resurrection to fully manifest. (See Acts 20:9–12.) So it was for Daniel Ekechukwu.

STIFF AS IRON

In Daniel's case, a full recovery required several days. The process seemed slow and uncertain, at first. After I left for the airport, Pastor Paul addressed the crowd of people who had remained at Grace Cathedral. He announced that during the service, the body of a dead man had been brought into the church and laid on a table in the basement, and that he was now breathing. As he was speaking from the podium, Mr. Ikugpe entered the sanctuary through a side door and interrupted him. He raised his cane—and his patriarchal voice—and said, "I am his father. It is true that he is now breathing. But he is still as stiff as iron. He has been dead since Friday and has been in a mortuary."

At this point, the entire pastoral staff was called into the basement. They gathered around the table and began to pray. The remaining security officers cleared the room and stood nearby, controlling the entrance and exit of curious people. Outside, a large crowd had gathered around the ambulance. Inside it, they could see the coffin lid and the two wads of cotton that had been packed inside Daniel's nostrils. Many of them snapped photos through the windows as they listened to the story the parking lot attendants told with awe.

Inside the church, Daniel continued to breathe. A pastor who had laid hands on his cold corpse when he had first been brought in now laid hands on his chest and announced that heat was returning to the torso. After a while, the assistant pastor led the group in singing hymns of praise and worship to God. For a couple of hours, they alternated between praying and singing.

TWO KINGDOMS

As he sat and watched the entire sequence unfold, Mr. Manu must have been reminded of the singing he had heard in the mortuary on Friday night. Mr. Ikugpe, too, had returned to the room to watch and listen. What they saw were Christians in action, not animists, and it began to dawn on these men that there were two spiritual kingdoms, and that these kingdoms operated very differently. One involved rituals, fetishes, blood sacrifices, incantations, and hitting a corpse with a Bible seven times, producing only death and darkness. Here, they were experiencing another spiritual kingdom, one that produced light and life and singing.

Nneka sat quietly beside them, her son leaning against her knees. All of her loud arguments were over. All of her weeping and pushing and fighting to see her dream carried out had ceased. She had been beaten in order to sit and witness this moment. She had been rejected, denounced as crazy, and deserted by everyone who should have supported her, including the husband now breathing on the table.

She did not need to say a word for the two men beside her on the bench to feel shame and humiliation. It was clear Mr. Ikugpe was no longer in charge. Mr. Manu was out of his element. Daniel was breathing, and she merely waited to receive the full manifestation of her promise from God. She had no doubt that she was about to become one of the women mentioned in the book of Hebrews who had received their dead raised to life again.

I had been gone for several hours when the atmosphere in the basement grew oppressive. Various people presented their special reasons to come inside, and, one by one, they were allowed to enter. In the heat of the afternoon sun, the room filled with stale air. Staff members took turns fanning Daniel's body to keep it from overheating.

Next, they observed rapid eye movement behind his closed eyelids. An assistant pastor suggested that they begin to massage the body. Since the heart was now beating, they felt that the rigor mortis might respond to their efforts. At first, they concentrated on his hands and fingers, which, as I have said, had been injected with embalming fluid; as a result, they were very rigid. One pastor took each hand and massaged it as they prayed and sang. Then they moved up the arm, rubbing it to encourage circulation. Daniel's hands began to loosen and became more relaxed. Encouraged by this progress, a pastor began to rub his neck. After several minutes of this process, one of the pastors placed his hand on Daniel's forehead and began to move his head gently from side to side. This procedure was filmed with a video camera. The stiffened body that Mr. Ikugpe had described to the congregation was slowly becoming limber.

AWAKE AT LAST

This continued until late afternoon. People began to sit down and have conversations around the room as Daniel's body progressed toward returning to life. Suddenly, Daniel sneezed and sat up on the table. The room exploded with screams and praises to God. People were crying, laughing, and nearly in hysterics. Nneka merely smiled and nodded. This was what she had expected. Daniel's eyes opened, and he began to look around in confusion. One of the pastors rushed to him and embraced him tightly, but he was unable to speak. His older son, who had witnessed the events of the entire day, rushed to him.

"Daddy! Daddy!" he cried.

But Daniel was emotionless, showing no recognition whatsoever. Nneka stepped in and comforted the boy.

The pastoral team helped Daniel from the table and stood him up next to it. He was quite unsteady on his feet. Just like his fingers, his toes were still curled from the injections administered by Mr. Manu. One of the pastors suggested that they take him upstairs to an office that had a ceiling fan. In their enthusiasm, they began to help Daniel toward the stairwell.

At this point, he spoke his first word. "Water," he said.

The procession stopped, and the room was searched for a bottle of water.

"Where is my file?" Daniel asked. "My file...my file."

Someone handed the pastor a bottle of water, and while everyone watched, he helped Daniel drink from it. The liquid seemed to revive his senses even more. The group continued to help him up the stairs, as if he were a toddler just learning to walk. When they reached the office, they sat him in a chair beneath the whirl-ing ceiling fan. Soon, the room filled with people, crowding in to watch.

Daniel Ekechukwu is assisted after being raised from the dead.

"My file," Daniel said again, seeming puzzled by the change of location. "Where is my file?"

In the crowd were the church staff members and their spouses. The air became as stuffy as the basement had been. It was suggested that they take him into the auditorium, because it was somewhat cooler, and the air circulation was better there. When they reached the sanctuary, they took him to the carpeted platform area and lowered him into one of the overstuffed armchairs that I had sat in prior to preaching that day. The video footage of this moment shows that Daniel was beginning to become more aware of his surroundings but was still looking confused, as if slowly coming out of a long coma.

A man had come to observe the miracle with his crippled wife. When she saw Daniel alive she threw her crutches away and began running around the sanctuary. Her husband threw his hands into the air and cried, "I am a sinner. I repent. God, please forgive me of my sins."

Seated beside Daniel, Nneka began to ask him how he felt. She recalled the fatal internal injuries he had suffered. After the accident, his every breath had been labored. She checked to see if he was breathing normally. She had him open his mouth and saw that his tongue had turned black. But as he continued sipping water and taking in oxygen, it began to take on a more normal color. The worst injuries he had suffered had come about when the steering column of the car had impaled his chest. That kind of impact is often enough to kill a man outright. It often will stop a heart from beating. It is a lethal blow that has even been incorporated into certain martial arts instruction.

Nneka Ekechukwu
comforts her husband, Daniel.

"Do you have pain?" she asked.

"Yes," he replied.

"Does it hurt where the steering column hit you?" She reached out and touched his bare torso.

"No," he said. "I hurt where those men massaged me. My neck and arms."

Nneka was amazed. Not only had he been raised from the dead; he had been healed of his injuries, so that he now suffered only the minor discomfort of sore muscles.

By late afternoon, though Daniel still seemed dazed and confused, he began to recognize his family members. He asked Nneka what the meaning of everything was, and she told him to wait until they got home, when she would explain it all.

As evening fell, Pastor Paul and his wife came to see them. They gave Daniel a shirt to wear. He acknowledged them but was not yet ready to communicate freely. Nneka told Pastor Paul that Daniel had died in a car accident on Friday and had been partially embalmed in a mortuary until that very morning. The pastor invited them to return to his home on the following day, if possible. He told them that I had ordered a camera crew from Christ for All Nations to come to Onitsha to capture the story behind the resurrection. The crew would come to his house and would want to begin filming immediately. He wanted to assist in every way possible.

Pastor Paul offered Nneka and Daniel a ride home that night and also said he would send a car the next day to bring them to his residence. They accepted. The ambulance was dispatched to return the coffin to the Ikeduru General Hospital Mortuary, where Mr. Manu would reclaim it and return it to his inventory. Mr. Ikugpe returned to Amaimo in Mr. Manu's car. Both animists had much to discuss on the seventy-mile journey.

HOME AGAIN

Back home at last, Nneka wondered if things had changed between her and Daniel. The unresolved conflict still hung like a dark cloud over her head. Would she be banished for a year for striking him? She decided to wait until he was ready to discuss it.

Daniel was able to walk, but with difficulty. He moved around the house, touching things that were familiar to him. With each passing minute, he became more normal and more able to carry on conversation. At last, he stopped to embrace his older son. The boy's face broke into a smile as he hugged him. He asked about their other son, and Nneka explained that he was still in Amaimo, under the care of their extended family. They would need to make plans to bring him home.

Nneka put the older son to bed and returned to the main room. Daniel began to ask her questions.

"Why was I not wearing a shirt in front of those people?"

"Do you remember the accident, my husband?" Nneka asked.

"It is not clear. I remember a hospital and an ambulance ride. You were there in the ambulance. Two angels came with us, but they would not let me tell you that they were there. Then they took me by the shoulders and lifted me out of the ambulance. One of them showed me heaven and hell, and then sent me back. I saw Reinhard Bonnke on a hilltop, and we both fell down a hole. I woke up with all these people around me, and I had no shirt on."

"They removed the shirt when they took you out of the coffin."

"Coffin?"

"We brought you to the church in a coffin. We dressed you for burial at the mortuary, but the shirt had to be cut in two because you were so stiff. Did you know you were in the Ikeduru General Hospital Mortuary since Friday?"

"No."

"We took you out this morning to bring you to Reinhard's meeting."

"I was only gone for fifteen minutes. It was not long."

"My husband, it was part of three days," she told him.

He was silent for a long time.

"Husband, I had a dream while you were gone," Nneka explained. "You came to me and told me you were not dead. You said you were unhappy that I had left you in the mortuary. You also asked me to take your body to Reinhard Bonnke's meeting at Grace Cathedral. Do you remember that?"

He listened carefully but shook his head. He could relate to nothing she described.

Nneka was troubled to hear this. The dream had been so real to her, and Daniel seemed to remember the things he had experienced while out of his body. Why did he not remember the message he had delivered in the dream? It had been the very thing that had directed her to the meeting at Grace Cathedral. She had believed it so strongly that she had resisted every other voice and had endured fierce persecution. Still, she had been mistaken to assume that Reinhard Bonnke would pray for her husband. Likewise, she had been sure Daniel would remember the details of the dream. But he did not.

"I am very hungry," he said. "Is there something I can eat?"

With his request for food, life returned to normal. Her role was the helper of her husband. It had always been a privilege to prepare food for him. She took him into the kitchen, then opened the refrigerator and began selecting food that she knew he would enjoy.

Daniel noticed the abundance of food inside the refrigerator. He remembered the pride he had felt when he had purchased this appliance for his wife. It was an item enjoyed by few women in Onitsha, and it had been another sign of his success as the provider for his family. But as Nneka prepared his first meal since Friday, he saw the refrigerator in a new way.

He sat down at the table. "My wife," he said.

She turned to look at him.

"Please come and sit down," he said.

"But I am making—"

"Just for a minute. Please, come sit down."

She turned from the counter and sat across from him at the table, watching his face carefully.

He looked at her as with a pair of new eyes. "Nneka, my wife, if you ever need forgiveness from me ever again, from this day forward, I promise you, it is like food in the refrigerator. You come and get it. The door will always be open."

Needless to say, the meal was delayed by a session of tears and embracing between a husband and a very happy wife.

AFTERMATH

10

AFTERMATH

The day after Daniel's resurrection, he and Nneka visited the home of Pastor Paul NwaChukwu, as planned. As they related their story to him and his family, Paul was amazed at the strong smell of formaldehyde still emanating from Daniel's body. Nneka pulled up Daniel's pant legs so that the camera crews could capture the incisions that had been made for embalming. In fact, the chemical smell lingered on Daniel for many days as our cameramen followed the couple, retracing the path that had led them to Grace Cathedral. For weeks afterward, Nneka carried a cloth to soak up the chemicals as they sweat from Daniel's skin.

At the family compound in Amaimo, Daniel's extended family members flocked to see the brother who had been dead and was now alive again. His father had not been able to stop talking about the resurrection that he had witnessed with his own eyes. Some of the wives and brothers and sisters swooned at Daniel's feet when they met him for the first time since his death. As they hugged him, many stopped and held their noses because of the chemical smell.

As Daniel tells it today, he never had to preach to his father again. Mr. Ikugpe, patriarch of the clan, literally sat at his feet. He asked to know the God his son served—the true God who had raised him from the dead. After accepting Jesus as his Savior, he assembled all of the fetishes, potions, and books of witchcraft in the household, then had kindling for a bonfire assembled at the center of the family compound. As everyone sang hymns, he tossed these works of darkness into the flames. In the light of this fire, friends and family members worshipped the only true God in a celebration of new life.

In these scenes, Nneka saw the fulfillment of her promise from the book of Isaiah: "*The sons also of them that afflicted thee shall come bending unto thee; and all they that despised thee shall bow themselves down at the soles of thy feet; and they shall call thee, The city of the* LORD, *The Zion of the Holy One of Israel*" (Isaiah 60:14).

After the resurrection, the pagan mortician, Mr. Manu, gave his life to Christ. He eventually went to Bible college and became an evangelist. He is now preaching the gospel in Africa and sharing Daniel's resurrection story wherever he goes.

Dr. Josse Anuebunwa, the doctor at St. Eunice's Clinic, is a Catholic believer. Our crew filmed him meeting Daniel for the first time, just days after he had issued the death certificate bearing his signature. He was amazed and called it shocking to see a man he had declared dead now alive. "To God all glory should go," he said.

WITCHES IN VIENNA

Shortly after our crew had finished filming in Nigeria, they sent video clips to me for review. I could see that the story was absolutely amazing, filled with many details that confirmed the claim of resurrection. Early in 2002, I had scheduled a Fire Conference in Vienna, Austria, and I invited Daniel to come and give his testimony. It was absolutely electrifying to hear the story from the man who had been partially embalmed and spent the better part of three days in a mortuary. The crowd was spellbound.

Afterward, a man approached Daniel with a special request. He asked if he would come and speak at another event taking place in Vienna at the same time. It turned out that while we were holding our meeting there, the annual Esoteric Fair was in progress at another venue. This meant that shamans and witch doctors from around the world had gathered with crowds of people embracing alternative medicine. For several days, they would explore the interface between the physical and the spiritual world. The news of Daniel Ekechukwu's resurrection had already circulated throughout the networks of esoteric belief and practice. Of course, you might call this mere coincidence; but I would call it divine appointment.

We knew that the Esoteric Fair would be filled with those who did not know that there were two spiritual kingdoms at war with one another. The attendees had no clue that one kingdom had declared victory over the other through the resurrection of Jesus Christ. The man from the conference told Daniel they were willing to change their schedule for the opportunity to hear from a man who had been dead for three days and was now alive. Daniel brought the request to me for advice.

Well, I am an evangelist. What do you think I told him? "Go, Daniel! Go, and tell them your story. Then, preach the message of the gospel and give an altar call, right there in the middle of the Esoteric Fair. This is a door of opportunity for the gospel."

I must admit to feelings of jealousy. How I wished they had asked me to preach to that crowd. But their interest was fully aroused by Daniel's resurrection story. Naturally, they wanted to hear from him. I could hardly wait to hear of their response.

Daniel went and preached. When he returned to the Fire Conference, I called him to the platform. In front of our crowd, I asked him what had happened. He said that he had testified, preached, and given an altar call. Eighty witches and shamans had come forward to accept Jesus Christ as Savior. Hallelujah!

AMAZING FAITH

Daniel Ekechukwu poses with his own death certificate.

At the final service of our meeting, Daniel presented me with his death certificate. He said that he wanted me to have it, to always remember what happened in Onitsha. I thanked him for his generosity, but I did not feel right about receiving the gift. I held up the certificate and read it aloud to the crowd. Then I said to Daniel, "No, Daniel, this death certificate does not fit on my wall. You and Nneka should hang it on your wall at home. It is proof of the mighty miracle the Lord has done in your life, and a reminder of Nneka's amazing faith to see it through."

After the meeting, I had the certificate framed and sent to them, but not before I took a picture of it—a picture that remains in my records to this day.

NNEKA'S REWARD

In the months and years that followed, Daniel was invited to speak of his resurrection at events around the world. Nneka traveled with him whenever she was able to arrange proper care for their children, who now number four. Whenever he speaks, Daniel always gives Nneka the opportunity to share her side of their story. He has remained very vocal about the fact that his miraculous resurrection would not have happened without the faith and actions of his amazing wife. Together, they speak of the need to live in a constant state of forgiveness—to forgive others, just as we have been forgiven by God. The promise Nneka received from God in the vision of her ministering hand in hand with her husband has come to pass.

Christ for All Nations produced and made hundreds of thousands of copies of the DVD documentary, *Raised from the Dead*, which have circulated around the world. Through this story, more lives have been touched for all eternity than we will ever know on this side of heaven.

I recall one pastor of a megachurch in the United States calling me to say that he had shown the video to his congregation. At the end of the video, I preach a short salvation message in which I invite viewers to receive Jesus as Savior. After my invitation, that pastor gave an altar call. "We have never seen such a response in all our years of ministry," he said. That pastor went on to order nine thousand copies of the DVD for distribution as witnessing tools in his congregation.

My staff received a call from another American pastor who had been flying back from a mission trip to India when a flight attendant told him that she had been a Hindu but had become a Christian believer after seeing *Raised from the Dead*. Before meeting that woman, this pastor had never heard of Reinhard Bonnke or Christ for All Nations. Wanting to witness for himself what had worked so powerfully in the life of that flight attendant, he had then purchased several copies of the DVD.

We hear stories like these again and again, too numerous to list, as we continue to distribute the DVD around the world. Our point in telling about this miracle is to bring people to a saving knowledge of Jesus Christ. I am gratified to have played a small role in seeing this happen.

DANIEL'S FILE

11

DANIEL'S FILE

S o far, we have followed a trail of evidence that can be verified and put to the test. In fact, the elements of this miracle have been put to many tests. The people and places involved with Daniel's death, embalming, and resurrection from the dead have been located and questioned by many investigators, many times. Their findings compose a mounting body of evidence that points to the fact that Daniel was declared dead on November 30, 2001, and raised to life again on December 2, 2001, at Grace Cathedral in Onitsha, Nigeria.

However, as we endeavor to describe Daniel's out-of-body trip to heaven and hell, we enter a different kind of territory. The things Daniel saw and heard in this part of the story cannot be verified. We cannot visit the places he visited; we cannot speak to the angel who guided him there.

The details he describes are subject to the unique perception and recollection of his own mind. This is true for anyone who reports such happenings, and in every case, there comes a point at which the person who has visited another realm says, "There are no words to adequately describe it."

I think, however, that it is amazing to notice the many similarities between Daniel's account and those of others who have reported such things. In fact, we have similar descriptions recorded in the Bible. I do not doubt that people who die, or are near death, sometimes experience out-of-body travels into other dimensions of reality, where they encounter supernatural beings who really exist.

DANIEL'S JOURNEY

The point at which Daniel's experience departed from Nneka's was during the ambulance ride to Owerri. As he began to die, he says, he looked up and saw two angels—pure white beings—inside the vehicle, behind his wife. They glowed and were clothed in white. Their clothing and their flesh seemed to be of one substance. One of the angels placed his finger to his lips, as if to say that Daniel should not mention their presence to Nneka. He got the impression that if he were to tell her about the angels, she might become unduly alarmed. So, Daniel began to give her instructions about caring for the children and the church after he was gone. He felt happy to be dying. The pleasant sensations that went with the experience made it easy to leave everything, and everyone, behind.

The two angels then took him by the hands and lifted him out of his body. They turned and hovered above the ambulance with him, and he could see clearly through the roof. He saw and heard Nneka praying desperately over his body, saying, "No, no, no! You will live and not die, in Jesus' name."

He noticed that his earthly body was splattered with blood and badly damaged. There was an oxygen tube in his nose and an IV in his arm. By contrast, his spirit-body seemed to be in perfect order. He was happy to be free of his old, familiar body below. The two angels took him to a third angel, who told him that there were places for him to see in paradise. The angel gave him a file and a pen and told him to take notes of the things that he saw.

They moved without effort. The angel had only to address a destination, and they were transported there. First, they visited a place filled with beings who were glowing white and looked identical to the angels. Daniel asked if this was a gathering of angels, but the angel said that they were human beings who had served God and kept their faith focused on Christ Jesus while on earth. The beings looked up and worshipped a light that was too bright for Daniel to look at. They sang, bowed down, and raised their hands in perfect unison. He opened his file and began to make notes of the details that he saw. He then made an effort to join the worshippers, but the angel prevented him, saying that there were others things to see.

Next, the angelic guide took Daniel to visit the mansions that Jesus mentioned in John 14:2: *"In my Father's house are many mansions."* At first, Daniel thought that they were made of glass. But a closer inspection revealed that they were fashioned of some sort of gold. The floors seemed to be made of light. He wrote feverishly about the various wonders of these buildings, but he was baffled because they were strangely quiet and empty. The angel explained that the heavenly mansions were ready, but the saints of God are not.

THE GATES OF HELL

Next, Daniel was taken to a large archway with massive doors. Over the top of it was written "Welcome to the Gate of Hell." He saw no hinges or handles on the doors. The angel made a motion with his arm, and the gates rolled open with a deafening roar. Inside, he was met by a hurricane of torment. He saw a sea of humanity writhing in agony. The skin of all the people, no matter their race, seemed to be any one of a variety of shades of black. Some were clothed; some were naked. They were wailing, rolling, shouting, and gnashing their teeth. They saw him but not the angel. Some cried out to him for help, but he was merely a visitor, helpless to do anything but make notes in his file.

The people seemed to be suffering from things they had done on earth that now haunted them in hell. One man called Daniel by name and said that he, too, was a preacher from Nigeria, and that he had stolen money from the church. He promised that if Daniel would help him get out of hell, he would gladly refund all of it. Daniel was reminded of Matthew 7:22–23: *"Many will say to me in that day, Lord, Lord, have we not prophesied in thy name?…Then will I profess unto them, I never knew you: depart from me, ye that work iniquity."* Daniel saw no fire in hell, but the people in torment acted as if they were inside flames of fire. The horrors of the place were beyond his descriptive abilities.

SENT BACK

The angel then told him that he was being given another chance—being sent back to earth. The angel added that Daniel would serve as a last warning to this generation. He then was swept into a kind of black tunnel that took him downward. He sneezed and woke up in the basement of the church, hearing my voice through the loudspeakers in Grace Cathedral as I preached to the audience in the sanctuary. Thus ended Daniel's trip to the afterlife.

With these descriptions of his out-of-body experience, we can understand why Daniel began to ask for his file immediately after regaining consciousness. He was distressed to suddenly find himself without it. He had just come from recording the details of heaven and hell, as he had seen them. Now, he suddenly found himself naked from the waist up, lying in a dimly lit basement that was filled with people. He was being gawked at by shouting, praying, laughing, singing people, and was not really sure if he was in heaven, in hell, or on earth. No wonder he was confused. Nevertheless, he was very aware that he had no file of the record he had recently made, and, in his confusion, he began to ask for it. Many days later, Daniel gave up searching for the file. He came to believe that perhaps it had been merely a symbol of the memories he had collected during his journey.

Everything Daniel experienced while out of his earthly body seemed more real to him than the day in, day out reality of life on earth. Even though his earthly body had received healing, it did not have the same freedom of movement as his spiritual body. Given a choice between the two, he said he would choose his spiritual existence without hesitation. In the same way that his spiritual body disappeared as he reentered his earthly body, so too the file of information he had collected in heaven and hell had disappeared. It was left behind. Like others who have traveled to the other side of life's curtain, Daniel was left with only imperfect memories, finding himself at a loss for words to fully describe the sights he had seen.

THE THIRD HEAVEN

After hearing Daniel's limited descriptions, I think we all would like to have his file, wouldn't we? We all want to know much more about the things he saw and recorded in heaven and hell. I am reminded of the apostle Paul, who spoke of a man who was taken up from the earth into the third heaven—whatever that is. (See 2 Corinthians 12:2.) Every time I read this Scripture, I am gripped with curiosity to know what the first and second heavens are like. How are they different from the third heaven? And how many heavens are there? How we long to look into such things.

The apostle went on to say that he was not sure if the man about whom he wrote was in the body or out of the body, but he did say that the man heard things of which it is not lawful to speak. (See 2 Corinthians 12:3–4.) This is not the answer our minds want to hear. We want to know exactly what the man saw in the third heaven, just as we want to read the exact notes Daniel made in his heavenly file. Alas, it remains beyond our reach.

Again, the apostle Paul, who received so many exalted revelations that he was given a *"thorn in the flesh"* (2 Corinthians 12:7) to keep him humble, said, *"For we know in part, and we prophesy in part....For now we see through a glass, darkly; but then face to face"* (1 Corinthians 13:9, 12). It seems that every detail Daniel recalled about heaven and hell has left us with more questions that will not be answered until the day we see our Lord face-to-face. And just as Daniel eventually stopped seeking that file, so must we. Our walk is always *"by faith, not by sight"* (2 Corinthians 5:7).

SEEING THE INVISIBLE

12

SEEING THE INVISIBLE

In light of the resurrection of Daniel, it is still Nneka's faith that draws my attention. It continues to inspire me. She took action based only on hearing God speak in her heart. I, too, continue to act upon God's word spoken in my heart. Many times I have done this.

In every case, as I take action, there follows a trial of faith. It is a time in which the words I have heard remain inaudible to the world. To others, it appears I have followed a fool's quest. This is true for everyone who connects his faith to words like the ones that moved my heart in 2012: *America will be saved.* As we begin to take action based on this word, our faith will come under fire. This is the nature of our life in Christ, and His life in us. Faith is *"the substance of things hoped for, the evidence of things not seen"* (Hebrews 11:1).

On August 26, 2001, I preached at the Tata Raphael Grounds in Kinshasa, Zaire. At the close of my sermon, one of my team members said to me, "Reinhard, before you leave, there is someone you should meet." He told me this as he escorted me to the stairs at the back of the stage. As usual, I was drenched in sweat from open-air preaching in the tropics. My blood was pounding. I was still a bit out of breath.

"Who might that be?" I asked.

"A local pastor. He is from one of the churches sponsoring the crusade."

"Why haven't I met him? We had a Fire Conference for local pastors."

"There were too many. He could not get to you. Besides, at first, we didn't know who he was. He's someone special."

We reached an area that had been cordoned off for private meetings. Even in the backstage area at our crusades, crowd control is essential. We entered the area, and there I saw a small group of my team members standing with a fine-looking African pastor.

FLASHBACK

I knew instantly that I had seen the man before, but I could not recall the incident. His eyes were large, brown, and shining with a brilliant light. His smile looked like the full keyboard of my old piano accordion, except that his keyboard had one gold key—a large gold tooth shining in the front. He wore a well-pressed, double-breasted maroon suit with a silk tie of maroon and gold. He was trembling to see me, and yet I could not recall where we had met.

He seemed unable to contain himself. He rushed across the distance between us and threw himself to the ground, wrapping his arms tightly around my legs. He kissed my feet and wept with a loud voice. Gone was his appearance of dignity.

"Bonnke," he cried, "you saved my life. You saved my life."

"Who are you, man?" I reached down and took his arms, freeing my legs from his grasp. "Stand up here and let me look at you again."

He brought himself up and looked at me, tears streaming from his wonderful brown eyes. He said one word to me, and then I knew him.

"Bukavu, I am—"

"You are Richard," I whispered. "Richard!"

EVIDENCE OF THINGS NOT SEEN

The memory rushed back. Twelve years ago, I had seen him. I could not believe the change.

"Richard," I said, "last I saw you, there was no gold tooth, just an empty socket. You could not speak English, and you were filthy. You stank, excuse me, like an outdoor toilet."

I took his arms and pushed up the sleeves of his fine maroon suit coat and saw the evidence I remembered most—the scars. Yes, this was the same man. Tears spilled from my eyes. I embraced him.

"Richard, what God has done for you! What God has done!"

RARE BREED

Richard's story is so special, I fear that I will not do it justice. But I must try. I had last seen him in Bukavu, on the extreme eastern border of the Congo. Yes, it was Bukavu, 1989. How ever did we get there, to that far-off city?

Our journey had started, as I recall, with a scouting report. Such reports became necessary after one of our trucks sank in a river in the Congo. I don't remember which river it was, after thirty years of crusades, nor do I recall the exact year. Anyway, grand old Congo, known today as Zaire, is the most legendary country of Africa. It provided the backdrop for Joseph Conrad's classic story *Heart of Darkness*. Missionaries have told tales of the Congo since the days of Stanley and Livingstone. It is a vast land, three times larger than the state of Texas, with plenty of rivers big enough to swallow a truck.

I remember that our truck was loaded with gear for a crusade. It rolled onto a ferry and began the crossing. The rainy season had come early, and in the middle of the river, the ferry began to take on water. Down it went, with our driver inside. He managed to get a window open and escaped to the surface of the torrent, swimming for shore while praying for an absence of crocodiles.

Because of incidents like this, our team began to send out scouts in advance of the crusade ground crew. They would create customized road maps for our convoy to use. When our team traveled to any particular city, they would take advantage of our maps and notations to avoid hazards.

Our scouts traveled in Land Rovers equipped with chainsaws for clearing fallen trees. And since there are no "Mr. Goodwrench" signs on the fix-it shops in the bush, they carried every conceivable tool for fixing mechanical troubles on the back roads of Africa. Our scouts are a special breed of problem solver, and over the years, they have collected stories to fill a book many times larger than this one, believe me.

Whenever they travel, they investigate more than just road conditions. They check out the potential areas in the city suitable for us to set up our crusade platform. They log information about power, water, sewage, local police, crowd control, and any other detail that could benefit our planning team. There are a thousand ways to go wrong when conducting an African crusade; and, over the years, we have discovered them all. Our goal is simply not to repeat any mistakes. We have learned much, and our scouts are some of the most experienced and most fascinating members of our team. They have saved us untold misery, and we have not lost another truck in a river.

CITY IN NEED

In the late 1980s, a scouting team searched the back roads of the far eastern Congo. As they neared the Rwandan border, they came across

Bukavu, a city that was not on our list of potential crusade sites. Our planners had simply overlooked it. Nearly a half million citizens lived there, people who had never seen a Christ for All Nations evangelistic crusade. Furthermore, the scouting team had confirmed that the roads to the city were passable in the summer. Steven Mutua, a team worker, called me at our headquarters in Frankfurt.

"Nobody comes to Bukavu, Reinhard," he said excitedly. "We will see tremendous results. It will be glorious."

Nothing makes my heart beat faster than preaching the gospel in new territory. This began with my first assignment in the gospel-hardened land of Lesotho, in the southern part of Africa, in 1969.

"Begin planning a crusade in Bukavu," I ordered. "Steven, you will be in charge."

In July 1989, I flew there to preach. My team escorted me to the hotel where I would be staying. The next day, as I do for every crusade, I asked to be driven around the city. Steven had been preparing this event for months, and I wanted him to show me the local community. I wanted to hear from him all that he had learned about the history and lore of Bukavu. We took a local interpreter with us, so that we could interview people in the marketplaces and neighborhoods as we passed through.

A PLACE OF FEAR

At one point during the tour, we came to a prison. It was really more of a cage for humans near the edge of the city. There were no cells, just a large brick room with a prison yard attached, surrounded by bars and razor wire. Many of the prisoners were in the yard, taking in sunshine and exercising in the open air. A crowd of people stood near the iron bars bordering the yard. Steven stopped the car and turned the engine off.

"Who are those people outside of the prison yard?" I asked.

"Those are family members. If they don't feed the men inside, they will die of starvation. The government makes no provision for feeding men they intend to kill."

"All these prisoners will die?"

"All of the ones you see in shackles are condemned to die."

I could see a number of men walking around dragging heavy chains shackled to their arms and legs.

Steven pointed to a large tree with heavy spreading branches outside the yard. "Every month, a hangman comes from Kinshasa. The hangman earns his living the old-fashioned way. There is no scaffold. The condemned men are brought out to the tree, and a rope with a hangman's noose tied to the end is thrown over the big branch. The people are invited to watch, and many do. It is not a merciful hanging, like in movies about the Old West, where there is a long drop that breaks the neck. Each condemned man in this prison must move forward, one by one, as the noose is placed around his neck. Then the hangman uses the trunk of the tree for leverage to lift the man up, and he ties the rope off until the kicking and choking stops. Then, he lets the body down and goes to the next man."

"Have you seen this?"

"I have seen it."

"Can you imagine being one of the condemned, forced to watch what is in store for you?"

VISIBLE EVIL

"That is not all," Steven continued. "When a man is cut down, the hangman hacks off his hands and feet with an ax so that the shackles can be removed. Unless the family comes to claim it, the body is tossed onto a cart and dumped in an unmarked grave."

"Why doesn't the hangman simply unlock the shackles? Why go to the extreme of cutting off the hands and feet?"

"Because there is no lock. When a condemned man is brought here, he is taken to a blacksmith shed over there, and shackles are welded shut on his arms and legs."

"How do they do that without burning the flesh?"

"The men receive horrible burns. It is part of the punishment. They are considered to be dead already, and no one cares to take care of them. Some have actually died of infections that set into the burns before they could be hung. The empty shackles taken from a dead man are opened with a cutting torch and prepared for the next condemned man. And on it goes."

CRUEL AND UNUSUAL

I had seen similar prisons in other places in Africa. Once again, I realized that an African prison was a place to be feared. Unlike in Western nations, in this remote part of the world, "prisoner's rights" were unheard of. There was little public scrutiny of the justice system. Political leaders were appointed, not elected. The people in power were expected to dominate the population through fear and intimidation. I had met many leaders in Africa who used the prison system to get rid of potential rivals and political enemies. Justice was often miscarried. It reminded me of what prison life must have been like in the days of Paul and Silas.

"Here is the good news," Steven offered. "I've been visiting here, and several of the condemned men have accepted Jesus. I've been having a Bible study with them for several weeks now."

"Praise God, Steven," I said. "I want to meet them. Take me inside."

PRISON SONG

When we exited the car, a strange sound came to my ears. It was the rhythmic jangle of chains mingled with the chant of male African voices.

Steven looked at me with a knowing smile. "Those are your brothers."

"What are they doing?"

"They are singing songs of praise to Jesus—songs we taught them. They are using the only musical instruments they have."

"Their chains," I whispered, with realization.

I stood there and listened, and as I did, I sensed Someone else listening with me. As the sound of that wonderful, haunting chant rose in the humid air, I sensed a door standing open, straight into the throne room of God. I could almost see the great archangels at the portal of heaven, standing to receive this sacrifice of praise. My spirit flew like a bird from a cage, and I sensed that something wonderful was about to happen.

Steven approached the guards and explained who I was, and then we were allowed inside. The song continued.

I was appalled by the conditions in the cell. The men slept on filthy mattresses scattered about on the floor of that large cement-block room. The place was crawling with vermin. Buckets of sewage were gathered to one side. Clouds of flies swarmed over them. In the stifling heat, none of us could escape the stench. And the song, that wonderful chant of praise, continued to rise to the Lord with the jangle of chains.

We went out into the yard. Immediately, several men in shackles gathered around us. Steven spoke through the interpreter, explaining who I was. I greeted them briefly, but I was looking for the singing men.

MUSIC TO THE EARS

I saw them, about thirty in all, sitting in a circle. They were singing and swaying to the music. Their leader was a man of average build with a big smile that showed he was missing a front tooth. He rattled his chains with a flourish, like a choir director in a big church. If I had truly seen with the eyes of the Spirit, I might have seen him wearing a fine maroon suit, and smiling past a gold tooth. The minute I saw him, the Holy Spirit spoke to me, *Tell that man he will be set free.*

Lord, pardon me, I silently replied, *but it would cruel and unusual to say anything like that to a condemned man if there was any chance that I heard You wrongly just now. Please, say it again—more slowly this time.*

Tell that man he will be set free.

FAITH SPEAKS

We were introduced to the group of condemned men. I greeted the brothers who had accepted the Lord in the name of Jesus. Then, through the interpreter, I gave the whole group a sermon on salvation. A few of them responded, accepting Jesus for the first time. I then encouraged them in the Lord.

After that, I turned to Steven. "Tell that man who was leading the singing that I would like to speak to him in private."

Steven went to the man and explained my request. He brought him to me, with the interpreter. We walked to a vacant area in the yard.

"Reinhard," Steven said, "this man's name is Richard."

It was an honor to shake his shackled hand. "Tell Richard that the Lord has spoken to me today. The Lord says that he will be set free."

The interpreter hesitated.

I nodded. "Repeat my words exactly," I said.

He cleared his throat and then spoke to the man in his native tongue.

The man reacted, looking away toward the hanging tree. When he looked back at me, his eyes were filled with tears. He spoke through the interpreter, "Three times, I have waited in line. Three times, the hangman has become too tired to hang me. The last time he was here, I was the next man to die. The hangman glared at me like he wanted to see me dead. Then he threw up his hands and went home."

"Jesus preserves you, Richard," I said. "And now He says you will be set free."

JUSTICE FOR FEW

Richard listened. I could tell that he was still too afraid to reach out and take my word for it. Hope can be most cruel to a condemned man waiting to hang—a man who has seen the end of his life played out for him so graphically, time after time; a man who wears shackles welded to his arms and legs, shackles that he has seen removed only one way.

"What is your crime, Richard?" I asked him. "What are you guilty of?"

"Murder."

"You do not look like a murderer. Whom did you kill?"

He named the man.

"How did it happen?"

"We were in a bar, and a fight started."

"Did you start the fight?"

"I did not. But I did kill the man."

"Richard, if what you say is true, we do not call that murder. It is called self-defense, or manslaughter. Did you have a lawyer?"

Richard paused for a long time. He looked away at the tree again but said nothing.

Then the interpreter spoke.

"If the man you kill in self-defense is from a wealthy family, Reverend Bonnke, there are many in Bukavu willing to swear testimony for money."

We left the prison, and I never saw Richard again. I preached for several days in the soccer stadium to standing-room-only crowds of ninety thousand. The crusade created a huge stir in the area. Bukavu had never seen crowds like these in its history. Nearly everyone in the region attended at least one of the meetings. The number of registered salvations exceeded all that we had hoped and prayed for. We were ecstatic.

As I prepared to leave the city, I asked Steven Mutua to arrange one more meeting for me. I named a leading local politician whom I had met through the crusade. I will not here name the man or his office, because of the nature of the story that follows.

A POLITICAL SOLUTION

When we arrived at the politician's mansion, we were ushered into a waiting area. We were kept waiting for a long time. Waiting to see powerful people in Africa is something that I have learned that I must do. Finally, a secretary emerged from the inner sanctum and told us that the politician I wished to see was not available.

Now, if this were true, I thought, *they might have told us earlier, in time to spare us this trip. Either it is a lie, or they have decided the great evangelist must prove his Christianity by demonstrating nearly infinite patience in the waiting room.*

The politician was on a trip to Kinshasa, we were told. Instead of seeing him, we would be allowed to meet briefly with his wife. She would relay everything to her husband after we had gone.

After more waiting, a tall woman entered the room. She was dressed in finery and beautiful fabrics. I thought she carried herself with what must have been the imperial dignity of the Queen of Sheba. When she had made her entrance, an interpreter was provided, and I was able, at last, to speak with her.

After the formalities were over, I told her why I had asked to see her husband. I had come to plead for the release of a condemned man in Bukavu prison—a man named Richard. I described him to her, and I recounted his story of the crime for which he had been sentenced to die. I suggested to her that a competent lawyer would surely have made a case for self-defense. A good lawyer would have at least found a way to avoid the death penalty for Richard. Then I told her of Richard's conversion and of the way he led the singing among the condemned men in the prison.

She listened carefully to all that I said. Then she stood and excused herself. She said that she would see about what could be done, but condemned prisoners were never released from Bukavu prison once the courts had spoken.

After we spent another long time waiting, she returned. She asked that all of the other guests be removed from the room. At last, it was just the two of us. She stood before me, very close.

JUSTICE FOR SALE

"Reverend Bonnke," she said, "you are a very powerful man from Germany. Your organization is large, and your following is wide. You want my husband to do something for you. I would like you to do something for me. Do you understand?"

"Certainly," I said. "I will do whatever I can do."

"Do you have children, Reverend Bonnke?"

"I do."

"I have two children preparing to attend the university. Here, we have only the National University of Zaire." She shrugged, as if I would understand her problem. "It is not the educational excellence that you would want for your children, I am sure. And yet, my children have not been able to get the necessary scholarships to the schools we would choose abroad. I would like you to provide those scholarships, Reverend Bonnke. Will you do that for me?"

I was saddened, though not truly surprised. In a land where money could buy a death sentence, surely a bribe could obtain freedom.

"I am sorry," I said, "but this, I cannot do. I am a man of God. I will not make a deal to obtain justice of any kind. My answer to you must be no."

The woman instantly whirled around and moved away. I feared greatly for Richard. As she reached for the door handle, I nearly shouted her name. She stopped and looked back at me with an expression of shock. I pointed my finger at her.

"God has told me that Richard will be released. God has spoken. Do not stand in His way."

She left the room, shutting the door behind her with force. My meeting was over.

"Oh, Lord," I prayed, "save Richard by Your mighty power, not by the power of bribes and treachery."

I must confess, I departed Bukavu with a heavy heart. I feared that I had left Richard as I had found him—a dead man walking. But my fear was arrested by faith. It could not steal my hope that I had indeed heard God speak in my heart, telling me with certainty that Richard would be set free.

THE SUBSTANCE OF HOPE

Two years later, I was in Germany when someone reported to me that Richard had been set free. I shouted with joy to hear of it. To this day, I do not know what happened to trigger his release. Perhaps my words to the politician's wife had pricked her conscience; I cannot say. I know only that all the glory belongs to our Father in heaven.

Meanwhile, Richard began a new life as a free man in Bukavu. He told the pastor of the local church he attended that he wanted to go to Bible college in Kenya. He wanted to become a pastor, and he was determined to learn to speak English. When word of this got back to me, that was one scholarship I was more than willing to provide. Christ for All Nations paid Richard's tuition as he applied himself at Bible college. Years later, I heard the news of his ordination. I sent him my best wishes and congratulations, and that seemed a fitting end to it.

Now, twelve years later, in August 2001, he stood before me in Kinshasa, a sponsoring pastor of a Christ for All Nations crusade. He was wearing his double-breasted maroon suit and speaking good English, with his gold tooth shining, his eyes bright with the joy of the Lord.

We embraced again. I can tell you, this evangelist slept so very well that night.

Two long years of waiting had passed in this story before I learned about its happy ending. Twelve years had gone by when I saw it with my own eyes. How does faith handle it in the meantime? I have learned that when we speak the words that God has whispered in our hearts, we don't have to handle it—He does. Scripture says that He watches over His word to perform it. (See Jeremiah 1:12 RSV.) This means that in the trial of our faith, the battle is the Lord's. We find rest in Him.

AFRICA, SAMARIA, AND NOW, AMERICA

13

AFRICA, SAMARIA, AND NOW, AMERICA

One of the principles of my life is that I jump when God speaks. There is no need to sleep on it. When God speaks, it is always urgent. I rush to obey. As in the story of Richard in Bukavu, I have never been disappointed by obeying the voice of God. Likewise, on December 2, 2001, when Daniel Ekechukwu jumped out of his coffin, I jumped to the telephone. I knew God had made clear His answer to my prayer in the Sheraton Lagos Hotel: "Lord, this time I am asking You for a sign. I've never asked You for signs, but this time, I need a sign. If You want me to move to America, I want You to do something that I have never ever seen happen in my ministry."

That prayer was still fresh in my mind when I heard the words "He's breathing!" Soon thereafter, the miracle was confirmed. I telephoned my wife, Anni, in Frankfurt, Germany, insisting that by Christmas, we would be in America. In fact, we arrived on Christmas Day. The plane was nearly empty because so many had already traveled to their holiday destinations. We found a lovely home in Vero Beach, Florida, where we live to this day.

For a decade, Orlando has served as the worldwide headquarters of Christ for All Nations. The Full Flame Film Series was completed at Universal Studios and is still being distributed worldwide, as is the DVD about Daniel Ekechukwu, *Raised from the Dead*. As a result of the move, I have been able to speak to many more Americans, which has increased the number of our ministry partners. This, in turn, has improved our ability to conduct crusades in those places where the Lord directs us.

Since coming to America, God has introduced to our ministry Daniel Kolenda, a young evangelist with the same passion for the lost that grips my soul. God spoke to me to raise this man up to do what I do. And this, we have done. We are seeing Daniel Kolenda preach the same gospel and reap the same harvest that I have seen for so long now. In retrospect, the resurrection of Daniel Ekechukwu in Africa led directly to the raising of another Daniel in America—a man who happens to be my successor. It has been like watching pieces of a puzzle fall into place, one after another. And it has all seemed so satisfying and complete.

A WAKE-UP CALL

But the story does not end here. Imagine my surprise in the summer of 2012 when I learned that my decision to come to America was of far more significance than I had dreamed. In fact, I have only begun to understand it, because, once again, God has spoken of things that defy my natural mind. He began to stir my heart, saying, *I did not bring you to America so that America could be the offering plate for Africa. I brought you to America for America's sake.*

When I heard this, I was deeply touched and moved to tears in my prayer time. I never would have presumed that I might be chosen for such a purpose. The history of the United States, with its godly forefathers and inspired founding documents, cannot be equaled in the world. No other land has borne such fruit or produced such powerful ministries, including the worldwide explosion of Christian broadcasting. No other people have supported missionary outreaches with even a fraction of the resources from the church in America. American believers are the full alphabet of Christian generosity. How could I imagine that God would use me to preach to them the simple ABCs of the gospel?

But God said to me, *Every generation needs regeneration.* To me, this means the gospel must be preached, again and again. The previous crusades, revivals, and awakenings in the United States are not enough. The gospel must be received again in every generation. America is clearly a land in need of the preached gospel.

Much of the American population acts as if they have not heard the Good News. That is because the gospel must be presented clearly. Many churches have become so "seeker friendly" that the gospel has become disguised as just another self-help manual. But the gospel wears no mask. It is the power of God to save the lost, to deliver from guilt and from the crippling power of sin. The Holy Spirit has clothed Himself with the gospel. Paul said, *"For our gospel came not unto you in word only, but also in power, and in the Holy Ghost"* (1 Thessalonians 1:5). When the gospel is preached, the Holy Spirit operates in power.

THE POWER OF THE GOSPEL

Through hearing the gospel preached, people are led to a decision—eternal life or eternal death. Everyone has the right to choose, but the gospel is like breathing; there is no future in the alternative. Still, people need to hear it and choose for themselves: life or death. I tell them that only one way makes sense. I want people to appreciate the genius of the grace of God. I remind them that the God who created us also created the gospel. The very hands that formed Adam were violently pierced with nails on the cross. I want people to understand that only the sinless Savior could pay for their sins. In the garden of Gethsemane, Jesus faced the reality of our condition before a holy God, and He wailed in such agony that it nearly killed Him. (See, for example, Mark 14:32–39.) Creation cost God nothing, but salvation cost Him everything. The Son of God became flesh and allowed us to treat Him as the scapegoat for our every vile offense. This was done as the only way to reveal God's infinite love for mankind. How can anyone refuse such love?

I preach in order to help people understand that salvation is not a vague lovingness from a God beyond the stars. It is near, it is personal, and it is intense. It is the pen of truth dipped in the blood of the Lamb and written large across time and space. The gospel rings true in every generation, forward and backward through time, reaching even to the ears of the guilty pair hiding in Eden. In their shame, God sought them. In their nakedness, they heard the gospel when He called to Adam, "*Where art thou?*" (Genesis 3:9). God longs to restore the broken relationship. He seeks to save the lost (see Luke 19:10), and *we* are the lost children of Adam. "*For as in Adam all die, even so in Christ shall all be made alive*" (1 Corinthians 15:22). Hallelujah! To say yes to Jesus is to have our name inscribed upon the very heart of God, embraced to His bosom, from which nothing can separate us. (See Romans 8:39.) What a day of salvation we declare to the world!

VERO BEACH AND AMERICA

I asked the Lord where I should begin to obey His call to America. He directed me to my backyard. Literally, to Vero Beach, where I live. In obedience, I began to make plans for a crusade to be held in February 2013. I shook my head, thinking, *Well, this will be nice. We have a population of 14,000 people. Perhaps a few hundred will show up.* As the word went out, to my delight, sixty churches along the Treasure Coast, from Jupiter to Satellite Beach, agreed to cooperate. I was thrilled. God spoke to me again and said that what He was about to do in Vero Beach, He would do in a magnified way across America—city by city, stadium by stadium, coast-to-coast. It was then that I received the word from heaven that I had first heard applied to Africa so long ago: *America will be saved.* We saw five thousand attend each meeting. I declared the word I had heard from God, and as I preached the clear gospel, the Holy Spirit did His work. Hundreds were saved, and many hundreds were healed. In America, as in Africa, the power of the Holy Spirit is the hand in the glove of the preached gospel.

As I continue to declare that "America will be saved," I pray that you will respond with the faith of Nneka, not the unbelief of those around her. I will need an army of partners to believe with me in this great endeavor. Many people have already told me they think this idea is impossible. They say that America no longer cares to hear the gospel preached—that a nationwide revival in this jaded land is impossible. But I say to them that God specializes in turning impossibilities into possibilities. This harvest is not only possible, it is likely. For people of faith, the time to believe is now, before it is seen and everyone climbs on the bandwagon.

GOD'S SPEAKER IN SAMARIA

As I thought of a way to bring this book to a close, God opened up the Word to me concerning the biblical city of Samaria. This was the hometown of the despised Samaritans of Jesus' day. Jesus told the story of the Good Samaritan. (See Luke 10:30–36.) He also visited the woman at the well in this city. (See John 4.) In the history of Samaria, God illuminated two passages to me that contrasted the danger of unbelief with the glory of faith. The first story is from the Old Testament; the second, from the New. The first shows Samaria in riot; the second, Samaria in revival. In the same city, we read the story of one who bore the fruit of unbelief under the prophet Elisha; later, under the ministry of Philip, we see multitudes bearing the fruit of faith. The contrast is presented here for our instruction.

Historically, in the Old Testament, after the reign of Solomon, the people of Israel were divided into two kingdoms. Ten of the twelve tribes of Israel broke away from Jerusalem and established their capital in the northern city of Samaria. They built their own temple on Mount Gerazim and claimed it to be the true Mount Zion. However, they practiced idolatry, and their temple worship became mixed with pagan rites. They built a temple to Baal, yet God continued to deal with them. The ministry of Elijah and Elisha was directed to Samaritans. It is during the time of Elisha, who was God's speaker for that city, that we find Samaria in riot.

UNBELIEF SPEAKS

The Syrians had besieged the capital city. There was catastrophic starvation. Even cannibalism was reported. The citizens almost surrendered to the enemy. It was then that God's speaker, Elisha, was sent to the king with an unalterable word. But Elisha was not the only speaker in Samaria. There was a government speaker, as well. The royal officer, appointed to help the king, opposed Elisha when he heard his word from the Lord. God's speaker predicted that the next day at the same time, plenty of food would be at the gate of Samaria—so much food that a measure of wheat would cost merely a shekel.

The government speaker replied, "It is impossible."

Elisha answered his faithlessness, "You will see the food, but you will not eat it."

As we read this account in the seventh chapter of 2 Kings, we find that God caused the invading Syrians to hear the sound of a huge army approaching with chariots and horses. They became terrified, and, convinced that they were about to be attacked by a far superior army, they ran for their lives, leaving behind a well-supplied encampment.

When their retreat in the night was discovered, the king did not believe it. He was sure that the Syrians were setting a trap and would strike without mercy when the starving people came out of the city in search of food. He appointed his royal officer to guard the gate while scouts were sent into the enemy camp. As soon as the scouts announced that the camp was abandoned, the people of Samaria stampeded. They rushed the city gates and trampled the royal officer to death. Elisha's words had come true. The king's officer saw the food but did not eat it. The government speaker was trampled to death by people who rushed to receive what he had not believed in.

To me, this describes the terrible danger of unbelief. Yes, unbelief in every form is dangerous, especially when it stands in the way of sinners seeking a Savior. When it comes to the Word of the Lord, as Elisha proved, we must never say "impossible." Bible prophecy is history written in advance. That is how exact and correct it is. It is unalterable. God will fulfill His Word, to the dot on the last *i*. We must lay hold of it and stake our very life on it. When Samaria experienced a riot of faith, all unbelief was trampled in the rush to be saved.

ANOTHER SPEAKER OF GOD IN SAMARIA

Now we turn to the New Testament picture of Samaria in revival. In Acts 8:4–8, we read that there was a disciple named Philip. This was not the apostle Philip, who had been chosen by Jesus as one of the twelve disciples. Rather, this Philip was a deacon in the church at Jerusalem, chosen because of his faith and his being filled with the Holy Spirit. His job was to serve tables. What a humble task for such a man anointed by the Holy Spirit with faith and power.

After the day of Pentecost, the church in Jerusalem got off to a fine start. While serving tables for the growing congregation, Philip had heard the apostles quote the last words of the Lord: *"But ye shall receive power, after that the Holy Ghost is come upon you: and ye shall be witnesses unto me both in Jerusalem, and in all Judaea, and in Samaria, and unto the uttermost part of the earth"* (Acts 1:8). Philip heard this, again and again, and I can imagine that when he met Peter, he must have asked, "Peter, did Jesus really say 'Samaria'? Did He say 'Samaria'?"

And Peter would have replied, "Well, sure, He said 'Samaria.'"

Then Philip must have said, "If He said 'Samaria,' why is nobody going? Why don't you go?"

"Oh," Peter might have said, "our hands are full in Jerusalem. The Lord said 'Jerusalem' first, you know. Our work is so important here. We are spreading the gospel in the very precincts of the temple. Jerusalem must first get saved. Samaria will come one day."

Philip would not have been satisfied. I can imagine that he must have gone to John next. He must have gone to every apostle, one by one, and asked, "Did Jesus really say 'Samaria'?"

"Yes," everybody would have assured him, "Jesus said 'Samaria.'"

Then Philip made a quality decision. "If no one will go to Samaria, then I will go." The Bible records the stunning result. A big revival hit that place. This time, I don't speak of Samaria in riot; I speak of Samaria in revival.

Then Philip went down to the city of Samaria, and preached Christ unto them. And the people with one accord gave heed unto those things which Philip spake, hearing and seeing the miracles which he did. For unclean spirits, crying with loud voice, came out of many that were possessed with them: and many taken with palsies, and that were lame, were healed. And there was great joy in that city. (Acts 8:5–8)

How wonderful!

Did Jesus say "Samaria"? Oh, yes. Now it is obvious. We all say, "Oh, yes."

A SPEAKER OF GOD IN AMERICA

I heard God speak about Africa: *Africa shall be saved.*

Did He really say "Africa"?

My father was a pastor. I recall him saying, as I boarded the ship with my little family to go to Africa, "Reinhard, please, let Germany first be saved. When Germany is saved, then you go to Africa."

I said, "Dad, God said 'Africa.' He really said 'Africa.' Somebody has got to go to Africa, and I have said, 'Here am I. I will go.'"

And what about America? Did God say, *America will be saved?* Did He?

Oh, yes, He did. And He means what He says, because He always says what He means.

Every time I pray, I hear it ring in my heart. A mighty wave of salvation will roll across this land. God has not given up on America. Many think America has rejected the gospel. But unless you hear it clearly, it is not the gospel that you reject. There is a generation growing up that hasn't heard the gospel yet. We need to preach it to make it effective. The word *gospel* means "good news." News is not news when it is in a file on a shelf. News becomes news only when it is communicated. The power of God cannot be active when the gospel is kept on the shelf. We have to speak it; we have to preach it; we have to shout it. I have shouted the gospel across whole nations, yelling, "Jesus saves!"

One time in Germany, somebody asked why I shout when I preach the gospel. I said, "When I see how Satan torments our young people and binds them with terrible chains of fear, of guilt, of unspeakable perversions, with bondages and compulsions—when I see that, I cannot purr like a kitten. I want to roar like a lion. May the whole world hear it: 'Jesus saves!'"

THE ORIGINAL GOSPEL

It is this Jesus, and this Jesus alone, who will save America. This is the gospel I want to preach in these crusades. Yes, it may sound old-fashioned, but I have come to believe that if we preach the original gospel, we will have the original results. The inherent power of the gospel is salvation. And salvation will happen, followed by deliverance and healing, because it is the original gospel. Jesus went around doing good. He taught, preached, and healed wherever He went. Today, He continues His ministry through His servants—a ministry to teach, to preach, and to heal.

This is not the day of damnation. This is the day of *salvation*. We don't need prophets of doom and gloom. We need people who proclaim the good news. And the gospel is good news. Jesus didn't say, "Repent, for hell is near." He said, *"Repent: for the kingdom of heaven is at hand"* (Matthew 4:17). That is the glorious gospel.

Jesus didn't come to shame sinners; He came to save sinners. He did not come to say to sinners, "You are so bad and so wicked, I am going to give to you what you deserve." No, He bared His back for the scourge that we deserve. He took our punishment and our death sentence upon Himself. Jesus saves. This is the glorious gospel—the ABC of the gospel. I will preach it, and I need you to stand with me to pray and help us go from stadium to stadium in America's cities, as multitudes come to the valley of decision. (See Joel 3:14.)

I call upon all of God's wonderful people to join me. I know there are many of you who cry hot tears in prayer for God to save this nation. Let us come together in purpose. I call upon you all. Let us rally at the foot of the cross and do something.

Did Jesus say "America"? Oh, yes. He's got a plan to save the United States of America, as surely as He has a plan to save Africa. So, here is my hand. Let's join together; let's lock shoulders; let's march to the drumbeat of the Holy Spirit. Let's not doubt; let's trust God, and the Lord, who raises the dead and sets prisoners free, will do what He has promised.

God bless you, and amen.

ABOUT THE AUTHOR

ABOUT THE AUTHOR

Reinhard Bonnke is principally known for his Great Gospel Crusades throughout the continent of Africa. The son of a German pastor, Reinhard gave his life to the Lord at age nine and heard the call to the African mission field before he was even a teenager. It was there, in the small mountain country of Lesotho, that God placed upon his heart a vision of "the continent of Africa being washed in the precious blood of Jesus." Since the start of the new millennium, Bonnke's ministry has recorded seventy-four million documented decisions for Jesus Christ. He has authored numerous books and has spent several years developing the Full Flame Film Series, eight inspirational films aimed at inspiring and challenging the church to Holy Spirit evangelism. He is husband to Anni, father to Kai-Uwe, Gabrielle, and Susie, and grandfather to eight grandchildren. He and his wife now reside in Orlando, Florida.